FROM NEW AGE
TO
NEW CREATION

A Seeker's Journey of Transformation
from Darkness to the True Light of Jesus

MEREDITH SWIFT

Copyright © 2018 Meredith Swift

The content, formatting and design may not in any way be emulated, reproduced, duplicated or copied in any manner without prior written permission from the publisher.

Created in the Commonwealth of Australia.

Scripture taken from the New Spirit-Filled Life Bible (Copyright 2002), The Holy Bible, New King James Version, Copyright 1982 by Thomas Nelson, Inc. Used by permission. All rights reserved.

Edited by Palace of Writers Publishing
Book Cover Design by 100 Covers
Formatted by Jen Henderson @ Wild Words Formatting

TABLE OF CONTENTS

Introduction 1
Chapter 1: Of Love and Light 5
Chapter 2: Other World Adventures 9
Chapter 3: The Quest for New Age Nirvana 25
Chapter 4: Into My Heart 37
Chapter 5: Building Faith 53
Chapter 6: Resting in God's Promises 61
Chapter 7: Out of the Night and into the Light 69
Chapter 8: The Original and the Best 81
Chapter 9: Jesus – The Way, the Truth, and the Life 87
Conclusion 101
Asking Jesus into Your Heart 107
Dedication 109
References and Resources 111
About the Author 113

Thank you very much for reading my book!

You can visit my website and read my blog
at www.meredithswift.org

INTRODUCTION

> **Psalm 40:1** *I waited patiently for the LORD;*
> *And He inclined to me,*
> *And heard my cry.*
> *2 He also brought me up out of a horrible pit,*
> *Out of the miry clay,*
> *And set my feet upon a rock,*
> *And established my steps.*
> *3 He has put a new song in my mouth—Praise to our God;*
> *Many will see it and fear,*
> *And will trust in the LORD.*

Bogged down in the mire of a life where I often felt trapped by my circumstances, I had never truly experienced what it was like to feel free. I longed for that freedom. I longed to break free from my circumstances. I longed to be free to be myself and to know why I was here.

Why *was* I here? What was my purpose? The mystery of life was something I was fascinated by. I was drawn to dive into, and explore that which was unexplained, unaccounted for, infinite and unknowable. These were the spiritual dimensions that, for me, were far more real than the physical world.

The spiritual aspects of life have always been much easier for me to deal with than the physical, emotional and mental ones. For a long time, struggle and suffering have been my constant companions. You could say struggle is often part and parcel of being alive, whether it's big, small or in-between struggles. For me, the suffering came when I pushed against my circumstances. Struggles came when I wanted to be anywhere other than where I found myself to be or desired to be anyone else but myself. I wanted to escape from me, for it was painful to be myself, especially when I was around other people. I felt as though I simply did not fit in. As a result, I judged myself as lacking.

What I came to realise, over time, was that this perception of myself as lacking was a false one and a big lie! Rather than lacking, I am "fearfully and wonderfully made" (*Psalm 139:14*), I am created by God to "fit in"—only as *a unique* part of a bigger picture. This bigger picture is His good and glorious plan for my life—for my good and for His glory. And this wonderful plan includes forming a personal relationship with Him.

Who knew?

What follows on these pages is the story of how my life changed from one of *reaction* to one of *direction*.

Rather than having a constant reaction to circumstances, I now have a solid anchor in Jesus Christ and God's direction through His word and the guidance of the Holy Spirit. In many ways, there is still one thing that remains constant in my life. In this world we live in, I am still presented with a fair share of struggles and suffering. The only difference is that these struggles and sufferings do not engulf me anymore. They do not isolate me. And they no longer define me.

I first began to write this story I am sharing with you, in early 2016, before I wrote: *"Hearing His Voice: Meeting Jesus in the Garden of Promise – A Devotional Story of Encouragement"*[1].

---

[1] http://a.co/9L1nPZx

FROM NEW AGE TO NEW CREATION

Back then when I started writing, it was not easy. I reached a point where it became a real struggle to write the story of how I came to faith after being a devotee of the New Age. Then Jesus impressed upon me to *stop* writing this particular story. It was not yet time for me to do so. I felt upset and disappointed. But I obeyed—reluctantly—and put aside that story.

I knew God still wanted me to write a book, but I just did not have a clue what book I was meant to write! This is when He led me to write *"Hearing His Voice"*.

If you read *"Hearing His Voice"*, you will know the circumstances of how it came to be written. You will know how God used a time of great turmoil and distress in my life to provide healing, encouragement and blessing not just to me but hopefully to others as well. That's what God does! Scripture tells us that He works everything together for the good of those who love Him. And I find this to be true.

"Hearing His Voice" had been published for a few months when, once again, I set out to write the story you are about to read. This time, I got the go-ahead from the Lord Jesus. This time, the way the story is written is quite different from the original. However, the intention is still the same. The intention is to share how my life has been changed and transformed by my loving Creator. This in itself is so amazing to me—for the reasons you are about to see.

I share from my childhood onwards, to set the scene as to how my life has unfolded. Accepting Jesus as real has been a gradual process for me, even though I do believe He has been with me throughout my life—whether or not I was conscious of Him. I recount the experiences and circumstances which have shaped me, including "what" I have found with Jesus and how I have found it.

MEREDITH SWIFT

God wrote my story before time began; before I was even born. One day, my story on Earth will finish. Yet it will continue with God in the place where time does not exist. In Eternity.

So read on, my friend, and hear the story of one who was lost but is now found. Read the story of one who was once in chains . . . but has now been set free.

CHAPTER 1

Of Love and Light

__John 1:1__ In the beginning was the Word, and the Word was with God, and the Word was God. 2 He was in the beginning with God. 3 All things were made through Him, and without Him nothing was made that was made. 4 In Him was life, and the life was the light of men. 5 And the light shines in the darkness, and the darkness did not comprehend it.

A smoky haze from burning sage fills my senses. Darkness. The drum pounds, softly at first and then intensifies as it mingles with the beat of my heart. Claustrophobia threatens to overwhelm me but then gradually passes. I lay down on the earthen floor, hoping for coolness and relief from the heat of the fire pit. I am believing for my mind, body and spirit to be cleansed, refreshed and restored as I open myself up to receive the ancient knowledge, wisdom and whisperings from the Great Spirit. I surrender to my first "sweat".

It is 1993. Six soul sisters and I have come together, helping to build this sweat lodge with the intention for it to purify our bodies and our minds. By allowing answers to our deepest questions to come into our consciousness, we hoped to emerge from this experience with a fresh awareness of spiritual enlightenment. I was a seeker, looking for answers and cleansing for the darkness hidden within my soul. I was on a search for an antidote to the poison and pain of my past—not just of this life, but of "lifetimes before". I believed wholeheartedly that I was a soul having a physical experience; a soul that was layered with residues of "past lives", on its way to becoming whole and enlightened. I believed my soul was being born and reborn to parents that my soul-self had selected—according to what I needed to learn in a particular lifetime.

Experiencing a sweat lodge was one of many ingredients in the melting pot of my spiritual journey. I had been taught the sweat lodge was a part of North American Indian traditions, which in turn came under the umbrella of the New Age teachings. These teachings were the foundational belief system in my life. I was one of many people who found a measure of tranquillity and empowerment through this melting pot of various religions and practices aimed at finding self-realisation[2]. I had turned away from the church-going experience of my childhood, which I remember a little—wearing a white hat and gloves, sitting in a long pew, attending Sunday School and saying "The Lord's Prayer"[3]. From my past experience, I could not recall much about God—and even less about Jesus.

As the fourth of five children growing up on my parents' farm in the 1960s, my childhood was sheltered, safe and secure. Apart from almost dying of whooping cough as a tiny two-month-old baby, I was a strong and healthy child. I loved the freedom and space of living on a farm and spent lots of time outdoors. My brothers, my younger sister and I would pretend to be Cowboys and Indians with our cap guns, bows and arrows; or soldiers hiding in our makeshift forts, hurling dirt balls as ammunition at each other. As much as I relished the freedom of these outdoor adventures, I relished even more the freedom of the indoor adventures of my imagination.

---

[2] https://en.wikipedia.org/wiki/New_Age Accessed July 2018.

[3] *Matthew 6:9-13*

FROM NEW AGE TO NEW CREATION

The mid-1960s was an era of few toys and even fewer children's television shows. So, the fuel that fanned the flames of my imagination was reading. Books were my escape. My refuge. To me, reading was as natural as breathing and I loved nothing more than to curl up with a good book. The more fantastic the characters, the better. If these characters were part of the "other world"—the world of the supernatural—that was even better . . .

CHAPTER 2

Other World Adventures

Ephesians 6:12 For we do not wrestle against flesh and blood, but against principalities, against powers, against the rulers of the darkness of this age, against spiritual hosts of wickedness in the heavenly places.

Fairies and pixies. Unicorns. Ghosts. Vampires. Witches and warlocks. Time travel. Children who stepped up, despite their fear, to save their loved ones. Or to save the world. These were the characters who inhabited the books I liked to read the most. The seven books comprising the *Chronicles of Narnia* by CS Lewis were my absolute favourites, closely followed by *"A Wrinkle in Time"* by Madeleine L'Engle, *"A Traveller in Time"* by Alison Uttley, *"Elidor"* by Alan Garner and *"The Secret Garden"* by Frances Hodgson Burnett. All of these books were rich in depth, steeped in the imagery of other worldly landscapes and adventures.

I would become so involved with what I was reading that when I put the book down, I expected the events depicted in the books to just keep on happening. The veil separating this world and theirs seemed so very thin. And the other world of these books was so appealing! A world dripping with colour and alive with fantasy. I was inspired to live bravely like the children in these books. One of the ways I did this was by acting out brave and bold characters like the Coca Ninja, from one of my favourite TV shows "*The Samurai*"[4]. Jumping off roofs, leaping out of trees and fighting battles against stealthy adversaries became a part of my everyday life. I loved to push my body to the limit.

For instance, during school breaks, one of my favourite pastimes was seeing how high my friends and I could go on the swings. "How high?" we would ask each other. "Sky high!" would be our triumphant reply. I especially liked swinging on the trapeze swing. I would go as high as I possibly could, and only then would I let go.

Came the day, though, when I lost my grip—before I had decided to let go. Instead of landing on my feet on the grass as I usually did, I fell flat on my back onto the cement slab directly underneath the swing. Apart from being badly winded (unable to breathe) for what seemed like an eternity, I was unaware that I had done any damage to myself.

I had, in fact, sustained quite a considerable damage. Months later, after a full day swimming at a friend's birthday pool party, I could barely move due to the pain in my back. I was compelled to tell my Mum about this pain and she promptly took me to the doctor. X-rays revealed the results of my fall. My lower lumbar vertebrae were crushed and flattened into the shape of a butterfly. I had also developed scoliosis. Soon afterwards, another freakish accident (my brother pushed me off my bike and I fell onto the corner of our mailbox) caused me to fracture my coccyx.

I was instructed by the doctor to cease any strenuous physical activity, in case my back was harmed further. Outside play during recess and lunchtime was forbidden. This was so hard. I was blessed to have a best friend who would stay indoors with me. We occupied ourselves with activities like reading and drawing. We also held our own séances. A

---

[4] https://en.wikipedia.org/wiki/The_Samurai_(TV_series)   Accessed August 2018

FROM NEW AGE TO NEW CREATION

storeroom at the back of our classroom, containing little more than a small table and chairs, made an ideal setting. Seated at the table, we arranged the letters of the alphabet, "Yes" and "No" in a circle with a glass positioned in the centre. We would ask the "spirits" questions and, with one finger resting lightly on the glass, wait for the glass to move in response.

I don't recall exactly how many of these séances we had but they were a regular occurrence. They ended abruptly, however, the day the glass seemed to take off of its own accord. Needless to say, my friend and I were completely terrified by this. We never again held another séance. I do not remember why we had decided to become involved in this activity in the first place. I suspect that, even at the tender age of 11, I was searching for answers beyond the physical realm—and I had also begun to experience the dark forces which are a very real part of this fallen world we live in.

Another major change at this time was my older brother and sister having to leave home quite suddenly and attend boarding school. The Vietnam War had not long finished, and we had some teachers at our local High School who were conscientious objectors. One of these teachers had been jailed for resisting the draft. My parents deemed the High School environment too political, so they pulled my older siblings out. I found it difficult to cope with the sudden loss of my big sister, who was in many ways more of a mother to me than my own Mum. I retreated even more into my inner world, continuing to read my favourite fantasy/adventure/time travel books voraciously.

I loved words and everything to do with them—spelling, sounds and sentence construction—and one of the best presents I ever received was when my parents gave me a diary the Christmas I turned 12. Thus, began my lifelong love affair with writing. This love affair quickly progressed to a whole new level with the gift of a typewriter a couple of

Christmases later. I would spend hours on this typewriter and within six months I had written my first book. "*The Mind Boggles*" was a science fiction story set on the planet of Angostenma, whose inhabitants were enslaved by a fiendish feline called Maleficent. Two scientists met and fell in love when they journeyed to this planet. They joined forces to defeat Maleficent, got married, had twin daughters and lived happily ever after. This book has long since been lost but it is one I would dearly love to read again!

Reading and writing were my escape from the awkwardness of adolescence and the growing realisation that others were not like me. I was not one of the popular girls. At one stage I had no friends at all. During recess and lunchtime, I would sit in the sanctuary of the high school library and read. This was a safe haven, a welcome relief from the pain of rejection. Despite having no conscious recollection of faith in God during my teenage years, a poem I wrote in my diary at age 14 is evidence that I believed He was there. I signed this poem "Sad and Lonely", indicating my state of mind at this time.

> *"What one person can do for another person,*
> *Is beautiful,*
> *What one person can do to another person,*
> *Is terrifying.*
> *Why should this be so?*
> *I don't know . . .*
> *Do you God?"*

On the plus side, this time of introversion strengthened my character. My solitude saw me come to rely on myself and I became comfortable with being on my own. I came to realise that I did not need these "friends" in my life. Ironically, after this realisation, the rejection stopped, and my classmates wanted to spend time with me again.

FROM NEW AGE TO NEW CREATION

During my 16th year, my grandmother, who we called Ma, passed away. Ma lived in another state, so we did not have much contact with her. I remember her as a very quiet and kind lady. Her death devastated my mother, who had loved her very much. In the months that followed, Mum suffered a nervous breakdown and was hospitalised.

We did not know what the matter with my mother was and whether it was life-threatening. I remember visiting her in the hospital and asking her how she was. My Mum would reply, with a vacant expression, that she didn't know. This was an era where the focus on mental health and treatment was very limited. On both sides of my family, anxiety and depression were present. We were not a particularly expressive family and showing emotions like anger or sadness was discouraged. It was expected that, whatever happened, we would stoically soldier on. Needless to say, this was not conducive to being mentally healthy.

During this time, I took on the responsibility of keeping the house running. Making sure meals were cooked and the house was clean, I struggled to keep my schoolwork up to the high standards I had placed on myself. It was no surprise that I was soon feeling totally overwhelmed—so much so that I began to experience suicidal thoughts. I would regularly repeat to myself that I wanted to die. I never acted on these thoughts, but the sense of hopelessness ruled me as if I were in the grip of an iron fist.

This was the year before my Higher School Certificate (the equivalent to Year 12 now). I came out of this suicidal phase when my Mum's mental health started improving. Upon her return from the hospital, she had a new awareness of what she needed to do in order to protect her fragile mental state. Mum explored her creativity, learning how to spin wool, embroider and paint, as well as being careful to eat well and exercise. Most importantly, she had hope again! I believe this sense of hope filtered through to me.

MEREDITH SWIFT

My sense of hope was tested as I entered Year 12. Despite my parents being very understanding of the large study load demanded at this time, I soon developed a nervous disorder. My stomach felt twisted into unbearable knots and I was at times unable to eat or sleep properly. My only relief would come from lying on my stomach on a hard surface such as the floor. A family vacation, meant to be relaxing, was instead hugely stressful for me as I did not cope with the break in my study routine. I was relieved to come home and get back into the routine of school and study.

The hours of studying paid off, however, when I excelled at my HSC. This came as quite a shock to me, as I had convinced myself that I would only just be able to scrape through. I was named Dux of the school and qualified for University entry to Law School. However, at the last minute—being that my HSC year had been so fraught with intense anxiety—I decided I could not bear the thought of five more years of study. I elected instead for a three-year business/secretarial studies degree which I believed I was better equipped to handle.

What I wasn't equipped to handle was leaving home. My emotional fragility and immaturity meant that I struggled—big time—to cope and to adapt to a new way of life. I lived in a hostel with around 50 other students for my first year out of home. The weekly fee covered all meals and utilities. It was a rude awakening when, for my second year out, I moved from the hostel and into a share house with four other friends.

Money was very tight, and I was often broke. This was not just because of the costs of living. I had been introduced to marijuana and alcohol when I lived at the hostel and these were not cheap. But it seemed that the use of these provided a solution to my struggles with anxiety and low self-esteem. Marijuana and the occasional use of speed stimulants became my new normal, interspersed with alcoholic binges. Living in a share house meant there was always a constant stream of people passing through. Parties were a regular occurrence and my sole aim when I was partying was to get either completely wasted or blind drunk. Purely to try to cope.

Yet it was becoming increasingly impossible for me to cope. I had little inclination to reflect on the poor choices I was making. I did not want to concentrate on my studies any longer and I was failing my degree. My health was also suffering and, towards the end of that year, I had become very ill with glandular fever. I took leave of absence from my studies and went home to my parents to recover.

My recovery was quite a slow process but, after a few months, I was pretty much well again. I switched to part-time study and started looking for a job. This was not an easy process but, after applying and being rejected for countless jobs, I finally secured a part-time position as a Classified Ad taker. I worked as one of a group of over 60 telephone operators, mostly women. And I loved my job! I was the youngest operator and many of these women mothered me. Yet, despite feeling secure within this environment and coping much better with a reduced study load, I was still grappling with the depression that seemed an ever-present part of my life.

One of the women I worked with was a regular visitor to the Victorian Spiritualist Union (the VSU), which was part of the Spiritualist Church. She would seek guidance from the psychic mediums there. In an effort to gain some clarity and guidance for my own life, it became a regular occurrence for me to also consult these mediums. The information which came through from the "spirits" gave me hope and I felt that things were becoming clearer. The sense of hope and clarity I was feeling meant that I also began to feel better *about* myself and about *being* myself.

Being involved with the VSU opened me up to such things as conditions in the afterlife, clairvoyance, clairaudience, reincarnation, spiritual healing and astrology—all with the aim that the seeker would be brought to a wider and better understanding of life. Using these tools would enable the seeker to face anything that life offers and this would help them live a fuller life on earth. Lifted beyond fear and ignorance, the seeker could develop their full spiritual potential and fulfil their earthly mission.

Emma Hardinge Britten[5], one of the advocates for the early Modern Spiritualist Movement, originally received the principles of spiritualism through mediumship. Some of these principles were—

- That God was defined as a creative divine spirit of the Universe;
- The Universe comprised the unity of man, of spirits and spirit guides;
- That each man took personal responsibility for their actions;
- That there was life after death; and
- Each of these principles was open to an individual's understanding and interpretation.

I liked the idea of this sort of church! It seemed so alive and vibrant to me! I attended a number of church services as well as the sessions with individual mediums. Books from the church were available at the TS (Theosophical Society[6]) Bookshop, which soon became one of my favourite places. The bookshop stocked books which explored all of the areas the VSU specialised in. I was relishing these new influences and I felt as though my spirituality was blossoming.

---

[5] https://en.wikipedia.org/wiki/Emma_Hardinge Britten

[6] https://en.wikipedia.org/wiki/Theosophical_Society
All accessed August 2018

FROM NEW AGE TO NEW CREATION

Yet amidst this spiritual blossoming, my partying lifestyle was increasingly taking its toll on my physical, emotional and mental health. I was also supporting my younger sister financially and this was very stressful. By the age of 24, my depression had become crippling. As had been the case seven years earlier with my mother, there was not a lot of focus on mental health. My solution as a way of coping was to copy what I had seen my Mum do—that is, paying attention to my diet (I became a vegetarian) and continuing to explore my creativity—specifically, my writing. I began writing poetry about my journey with depression and found myself yearning for peace and tranquillity in my surroundings. Becoming increasingly disenchanted with the noise and bustle of city life, I was ripe for a change.

One of my best friends, Sally[7], had moved to a coastal town about 90 minutes away and was pursuing her creative dream to be a potter. I would visit Sally and her partner, also a potter, and revel in the beauty and tranquillity of the area they lived in. I found their creative lifestyle inspiring. I decided to relocate and pursue my own dream of being a writer—specifically, a poet.

I was able to provide for myself by finding a part-time job as a cook at the local hospital. My sister decided to move with me, finding work as a nurse aide at the same hospital. Home was a tiny one-roomed cabin with an outdoor shower and no power, set in the stunning beauty of the state forest. I thrived on the simplicity of my new life—writing in the mornings, walking the many bush trails surrounding the cabin in the afternoons, eating healthy vegetarian food and spending time with like-minded people. All of these ingredients mixed together were a recipe for the recovery of my mental health. My depression and anxiety decreased until they were almost non-existent. It wasn't too long before I

---

[7] Not her real name.

completed a book of poetry, which chronicled my journey through the depression.

Sally and her partner lived within walking distance and every week, at their home, we would gather for Satsang[8]. A group of like-minded spiritual seekers—on a search for "their truth"—would meet together. Usually, there would be a speaker who would give a short speech on some aspect of spirituality (for example, meditation or inner peace). Along with listening to or reading scriptures (however, not Biblical scriptures), there would be a time of discussion as to how this could be applied in practical terms to our daily lives. (https://en.wikipedia.org/wiki/Satsang)

I had found a whole new world of people who were focused on exploring their inner selves and who were striving to become "realised". Some of these people were devotees of the head of Siddha Yoga, the Indian guru Muktananda[9]. My first serious boyfriend, Lance*, was just such a devotee and I soon followed suit. Muktananda said: "God lives in you **as** you". We were all god, with a small "g". The realisation of the individual self as god was attained through meditation on the mantra "Om Namah Shivaya[10]" and activating the Kundalini[11]. In this way, I hoped to reach the ultimate goal of achieving self-realisation.

As part of this objective, Lance and I attended a 7-day chant at the Siddha Yoga ashram. I found this to be a confronting and very unsettling experience. Yet even though I did not like the chanting, I *loved* the meditation on the breath and embraced this with great enthusiasm

---

[8] https://www.yogapedia.com/definition/4997/satsang

[9] http://www.siddhayoga.org/baba-muktananda

[10] https://en.wikipedia.org/wiki/Om_Namah_Shivaya

[11] https://www.yogapedia.com/definition/4982/kundalini All accessed August 2018

and discipline. At around this time, I also became friends with Jenna*[12], who taught Hatha yoga[13]. I so enjoyed the practice of yoga and it was a great help in managing the pain of my childhood back injury.

I was reading books by authors such as Herman Hesse[14] and Florence Scovel Shinn[15]. Herman Hesse was a German-born poet, painter and author whose books generally centred on each individual's search for authenticity, self-knowledge and spirituality. Florence Scovel Shinn's series of books including *"The Game of Life and How to Play It"* and *"Your Word is Your Wand"* were my first introduction to the idea that I could pray to an "Infinite Spirit" who governed the Universe. This new practice added a dimension to my life that had been sorely lacking—that of faith, prayer and the purposeful declaration of what I wanted for my life. However, amongst my spiritual and mental growth, my physical and emotional life was a giant rollercoaster.

Even though I was journaling extensively, I was no longer writing poetry. My job as a hospital cook had finished and I began working as a barmaid at one of the local pubs. Once more, I was in a cycle of partying hard, drinking too much and behaving recklessly. By the end of 1986, in the grip of binge drinking and shallow sexual relationships, I felt compelled to move again.

Jenna also wanted to move, in order to pursue her dream of becoming a yoga teacher full-time in a nearby city. I was able to find work in the

---

[12] Not her real name

[13] https://www.verywellfit.com/what-is-hatha-yoga-3566884
All accessed August 2018

[14] https://www.nobelprize.org/nobel_prizes/literature/laureates/1946/hesse-bio.html

[15] https://en.wikipedia.org/wiki/Florence_Scovel_Shinn All accessed August 2018

Classified Advertising Department of their local newspaper. However, this turned out to be a difficult time as Jenna became very unwell with anorexia nervosa. We parted ways and I went home to live with my parents for a few months. Moving back to the city, I lived in a shared household with a couple of friends and worked as a secretary to the Head of the Social Work Department. Once again, I had a good income with which to pursue my interests. Top of my list was to explore my psychic development more deeply.

I stopped binge drinking, although I continued to smoke marijuana. As a balance to this poor habit, I ate healthily, meditated, practiced yoga regularly and exercised daily. I also enrolled in a holistic massage course. With my mental, emotional, physical and spiritual health much stronger, I began to have a sense that I wanted to help others. I believed I could do this through massage and alternative healing.

This was a time where tremendous spiritual change was occurring on the planet—change such as that described in the "Hopi Prophecy". An entry in my journal, dated August 17, 1987, describes the Hopi Prophecy as *"the beginning of the new millennium, a new power surge that will affect this planet from the inner heart outwards and will affect and raise the consciousness of all those that live on this planet. It will be the initiation of the 144,000 Rainbow Warriors who have been chosen to be the true leaders for the New Age. These leaders will be ordinary people from ordinary backgrounds but will have the compassion, wisdom and strength to help others along the path"*. I felt a surge of hope and excitement, mixed with a sense of urgency, at these words.

On the evening of August 17, there were "link up" gatherings all over the world. On that night I attended a party at the home of some new friends, a group of people who were into spirituality and psychic development. They were also into using drugs, in particular, marijuana and magic mushrooms, in the belief that they could expand their minds.

FROM NEW AGE TO NEW CREATION

One of the people in my new group, Ben[16]*, became my first real long-term relationship. Ben was a very attentive, kind and loving partner. He was a kindred spirit; a seeker wanting to live an alternative lifestyle and understand the self. Ben introduced me to the teachings of the famous Indian philosopher, speaker and writer, Jiddu Krishnamurti. Krishnamurti viewed the self as the source of all that is and was very much against religion per se. One of his famous quotes went thus: *"I maintain that Truth is a pathless land, and you cannot approach it by any path whatsoever, by any religion, by any sect.*[17]*"* I related to Krishnamurti's philosophy on life—that it was all about knowing the self—*my* self—and that organised religion was like a prison that needed to be broken free from. There was no *one* truth—instead, each seeker of truth had to find their *own* truth and express this.

Just before Ben and I got together, I had booked an overseas holiday with a girlfriend, travelling to London and Paris, where we were going to stay in an apartment on the Champs Elysee owned by her millionaire boss. We were to travel together for a month and then she was to come back to Australia. I planned to stay on as I had friends already living in London. I would find work and do some more travelling through Europe for around six months.

Falling in love was not part of my plan—but fall in love I did. Very deeply. I did not want to leave Ben. I had grave misgivings about going so far away and for so long, but everything was booked, and Ben encouraged me to go. Having travelled overseas himself, he did not want me to miss out on this enriching experience.

---

[16] Not his real name

[17] https://anaditeaching.com/krishnamurti-and-the-desolation-of-the-pathless-path Accessed August 2018.

I loved England and was particularly mesmerised by the abundance of old churches, some dating back to the 10th and 11th Centuries. I found St Paul's Cathedral especially amazing. Being a writer and captivated by poets like William Blake and John Donne, I was thrilled to find their tombs there. I also found the British Museum totally fascinating with its treasures of history such as the documentation of how early medicine was practised, based on the astrological patterns of the day.

Touring through England, I was also fascinated by the lay lines and energy grids of places like Stonehenge and Glastonbury Tor. As much as I loved experiencing and exploring these places, I was so miserable without Ben. Oftentimes, I also made others miserable with my moping attitude! I made it through four months, working and travelling around England and Scotland. I decided not to travel through Europe and cancelled the tour I was paying off. When I came home from my travels overseas, Ben and I resumed our passionate relationship. We quickly moved in together. The best of friends, we did so much together and rarely disagreed on anything. When we did disagree, we were able to resolve this through good communication. For over a year our relationship was very easy and loving.

However, cracks started to appear when I came to a point where I wanted to get married. Ben did not. An unplanned pregnancy magnified the strain in our relationship. Ben did not want our baby and so, very reluctantly and with great distress, I agreed to an abortion. To this day, this remains a deeply painful wound that is still healing. I weep for the loss of this innocent child—a child who I killed for purely selfish reasons.

I was still traumatised and mourning the loss of this child when, exactly two years to the day of the beginning of our relationship, Ben broke up with me. He needed "some space to sort things out". Just like that, the relationship which I had believed to be my forever was over, leaving me totally devastated. I had truly loved Ben and when he left me, I felt totally abandoned and unable to understand why he wanted to end the relationship. I still could not understand why he didn't want our baby. I was heartbroken.

I saw my heartbreak as going either one of two ways. I could either collapse into the heartbreak or let it drag me down into a state of helplessness and victimisation, wallowing in it and letting it become my identity. On the other hand, I could use it to fuel a new dream, propelling me into a remaking of myself, allowing it to be the impetus for me to rise like a phoenix out of the ashes.

I chose the latter. The phoenix rising out of the ashes. As a firm believer in astrology then, the phoenix rising out of the ashes was one of the hallmarks of my star sign, Scorpio. I needed rebirth. I needed to reinvent myself to deal with my heartache. And the way I did this was to throw myself further into my psychic development and the quest to realise who I was . . . and why I was here.

CHAPTER 3

The Quest for New Age Nirvana

***Ecclesiastes 1:9** That which has been is what will be;*
That which is done is what will be done,
And there is nothing new under the sun.
10 Is there anything of which it may be said,
"See, this is new?"
It has already been in ancient times before us.
11 There is no remembrance of former things,
Nor will there be any remembrance of things that are to come
By those who will come after.

Shortly after the devastation of my relationship breakdown in 1989, I attended an alternative healing conference where I met one of the most important spiritual teachers and mentors in my life. Dina[18]* and I partnered up for an activity at one of the workshops and instantly clicked. Warm, wise and caring, Dina and her husband had their own alternative healing business. I immediately booked an appointment for some healing work with her.

I felt inspired and encouraged by Dina having her own successful healing business working from home. I wanted so much to also achieve the same goal! I was certain this was the direction I wanted my life to go

---

[18] Not her real name

in. I wanted to create a safe and sacred healing space for women to get in touch with their bodies.

Author and healer Louise L. Hay's[19] little blue book *"Heal Your Body"* (1976) was my reference guide at this time. It detailed the possible mental causes of physical ailments—the connection between the mind and the body. I had already been exposed to this connection during my holistic massage course. I had learned that traumatic memories can be trapped within the muscles—as pain or blockages—and released through massage. I wanted my clients to be able to access what the pain in their bodies was trying to tell them—and to be able to release the blockage through the massage. Before the massage, we would talk about where they were carrying tension or pain. For example, if their shoulders were hurting, this could indicate they were feeling weighed down by responsibilities. The tension was like a guidepost pointing towards the issues which needed to be addressed in their life. During the actual massage, they could reflect on and process what we had spoken about.

I had set up a massage room in the house I had shared with Ben. However, I was forced to find a new place to live when the roof caved in—literally!—at the front of the house. I then moved in with a girlfriend and her baby daughter. After working as a Personal Assistant to a Marketing Executive for a year, I had gone back to my old job working at Classified Ads but was becoming increasingly disenchanted with their new emphasis on sales. I wasn't sure how much longer I would be able to cope with this.

Having been granted some compensation money for the roof that caved-in, I hoped this would give me an "out" of my unsatisfying job. The money was very slow to arrive. The day it did is etched clearly in my memory. Pausing at the top of the stairs which led down to the mailbox,

---

[19] https://en.wikipedia.org/wiki/Louise Hay

FROM NEW AGE TO NEW CREATION

I looked up at the sky and declared to the Universe "If you want me to do massage full-time, then send me that money today". I ran down those stairs, collected the mail and, sure enough, the cheque was there! Honouring my pledge to the Universe, I quit my job and began to concentrate on doing my massage full-time.

Money was very tight in those early days of my business. I worked from home, did mobile massage and worked at a couple of different Healing Centres. It was around this time I decided that, if I was going to get serious about being an alternative healer, then I also needed to get serious about being completely healthy. I quit my regular marijuana use and spent a difficult year withdrawing—eating lots of biscuits to compensate (not very healthy but it did the trick)!

After a couple of further house moves sharing with friends, I decided I wanted to live by myself. In 1992 I moved into my own place and became laser-focused on running my business. With no money to spare to have business cards printed, I handmade them instead and put them anywhere and everywhere that I thought might attract clientele.

I also took over another masseuse's established clientele when she was unable to continue with her business. It was at this time that I began consistently using creative visualisation as a tool to help my new business become a success. For example, I imagined my appointment book filling up and money being attracted to me. I did this whenever I could, and I also made a cassette tape (who remembers these?) of my own voice, where I recited a visualisation of money being attracted to me. I listened to this every night before I went to sleep—feeding my subconscious with the outcome I desired. Just as I imagined, my appointment book began filling up. Slowly and steadily, through word of mouth, my business was growing.

I also attended many different workshops—geared to develop my psychic awareness and sensitivity—on subjects such as reincarnation, past lives, auras and nature spirits. I studied aromatherapy oils and taught myself to read the tarot. Under Dina's guidance and mentorship, I studied psychic energies, visualisation, healing through crystals and sound and Native American Indian sage cleansing and drumming. I undertook Reiki Levels 1 and 2. I had felt a little uneasy when the time came to be "initiated" into the Reiki levels—Level 1 was basic and Level 2 advanced. All of the initiates had to have their eyes closed as the Reiki Master "fine-tuned" them and gave them the power to give Reiki. Because I didn't think a Reiki Master could possibly be untrustworthy, I pushed the thoughts of uneasiness away and went ahead with the initiation.

With Reiki 1 and 2 complete, I now felt qualified to begin to expand into alternative healing. Besides massage and alternative healing, I branched out into running workshops on the chakras and on "Manifesting Abundance", as well as holding weekly meditation/creative visualisation group sessions. All of my healing sessions and meditation groups would commence with an invocational prayer to "Great Spirit, God and Goddess, all that is." I did not stop to think what the "all that is" part might mean.

Channelling was the next progressive and natural step for me in my quest for New Age nirvana. Once again, I was taught by Dina how to do this. I wanted to attract a loving and kind entity and I wrote out this intention as an invocation. Then I would clear my mind and become like an "empty vessel". I subsequently began to channel a spirit guide called Jamil, who claimed to be from a planet that existed somewhere in the Pleiades.

I had been told by an astrologer that I had perfect planetary alignment to channel. This appeared to be true as channelling this entity came easy for me. I was able to "step back" in my mind and speak the words of Jamil. Every second Monday, over the course of many months, I was part of a group who would meet for channelling practice. I also channelled for other small groups of people and for individual clients. I certainly felt uplifted and fulfilled after these sessions. People responded very positively to the spiritual guidance offered by Jamil, often saying that questions were answered that they were thinking about but had not vocalised.

My ability to channel extended to my crystal healings. Dina had taught me all about the healing properties of each particular crystal and I became quite enthralled with this. I believed that I could communicate with the essence of these elemental spirits. I viewed them as beings who had the ability to facilitate healing within the energy field of the body.

As I journeyed deeper into New Age philosophies and teachings and applied them to my life, I found myself wanting to do better and be better. I felt fulfilled by the work and becoming the person I desired to be. I look back at this time in my life and there was no doubt that it was in so many ways very exciting and joyful. For instance, it was such an exciting revelation to me that I could create my own reality. By identifying my limiting beliefs and then re-programming my subconscious mind with new beliefs, I could achieve the dreams I desired. I felt as though I had found—and was fulfilling—my purpose. I was connecting with others who were like me—people on a spiritual quest to heal themselves and realise their fullest potential. I believed I had found my "tribe"—and we were all spiritual warriors with a mission to save the world!

New Age teachings were so attractive to me because they appeared to be steeped in peace, love and acceptance. They offered a way of healing the inner pain which was blocking the true expression of the self. In healing inner pain, a deeper understanding could be attained on the journey towards perfection and self-realisation. One of my favourite books at this time was Khalil Gibran's *"The Prophet"*[20]. Its messages of enlightenment such as *"your pain is the breaking of the shell that encloses your understanding"* were food for my soul, bringing me closer to answering the question of why I was here.

Every avenue I pursued in my quest for inner healing was, I believed, one step closer to this understanding of the truth of my existence. One step closer to *my* truth. New Age taught that there was no right and no wrong. All were merely perspectives and experiences on the journey to enlightenment. All were potentially useful to help me clear my "stuff" and heal my body, mind, emotions, soul and spirit.

All in the name of the self. My self. All about *me*.

Yet deep within my self, and always just out of reach, there was still this raw and aching wound that I could not bear to touch, and which remained seemingly unhealable. I sensed it was there, but it was so very deep that I was unable to pinpoint its origin—nor why it had the capacity to unexpectedly cripple me with the intense pain of longing and loss.

I thought if I could just do enough meditation, enough visualisation, enough affirmation, enough personal development and enough alternative healing, that this deep emotional pain would eventually dissolve. Surely, my complete healing of this pain had to be close! I did not realise at the time that my wound was one I could never hope to heal myself, in my own strength.

Four years on from my relationship breakdown, I had not fully recovered from the pain of my break up with Ben. I had since been unable to form another intimate relationship and for a short time, I

---

[20] https://www.bbc.com/news/magazine-17997163 Accessed August 2018

explored same-sex attraction. I quickly realised this wasn't for me. One other relationship during this time was short-lived. My yearning to find a husband and experience motherhood was turning into desperation.

I was in relentless pursuit of healing my past—my past not just from this lifetime but "other lifetimes". Even though financially I was prospering, emotionally I was starving. I was so tired of being alone. What was stopping me from being able to experience the love and happy marriage I craved? Was there something inherently wrong with me? Was I being punished for the abortion? In amongst this inner turmoil and anguish, I had also begun having memories and nightmares of being sexually abused, which took me off onto another tangent of what I believed I needed to heal. To this day though, I cannot say for sure whether these memories and dreams were real. They certainly *felt* real enough. Needless to say, I was in great distress.

The excitement and joy I had been experiencing in my life were waning as my list of alternative healing treatments was growing. I booked treatments for Kinesiology, Bach Flower and bush flower essence remedies, rebirthing, reiki healings, crystal healings and sound healings, Shiatsu, Rolfing, Bowen therapy, acupuncture, chiropractic, homeopathy, reflexology, deep tissue massage, Iris therapy and iridology, shamanic drumming and healing and Balance for Life. I had floatation tank sessions, undertook Inner Child work, past life therapy, timeline therapy, Alpha relaxation, guided relaxation and visualisation, psychic readings, tarot readings and Medicine Card readings. I was in constant consultation with my spirit guides and gained guidance from the runes, the I-ching, angel cards and dream cards. I read countless self-help books. Phew!

I was bouncing from one thing to the next. Feeling fragmented and in pieces, my anxiety was leading me into that dark place I thought I would never be in again. At one point, I was hearing voices inside my head. I desperately needed help for what was going on with my mind. Thankfully, counselling was by this time becoming quite commonplace. A good friend recommended a psychotherapist who specialised in working with dreams. I dreamed very vividly so this really appealed to me.

The kindness and compassion of this therapist had me bursting into tears at the end of the first session because of the care and respect she showed to me. Her work with me was very profound because for the first time I came into contact with the idea that our childhood experiences can greatly impact our adulthood. It was no longer about past lives for me. It was now about dealing with and resolving the issues of *this* life. I was getting back in touch with reality.

During this time my financial prosperity continued to increase and, as part of trusting the Universe to provide, I rarely counted how much money I made. I would just put it into my wallet and spend what I needed. I always had more than enough for my needs and wants. I decided to take six weeks off over the Christmas and New Year period and travel to Nepal.

I wanted to trek in the Himalayas as well as undertake a silent Buddhist meditation retreat. I had seen the Dalai Lama[21] when he came to my city and I felt inspired by him and by the principles of Buddhism. A friend of a friend at the time lived and served at the Nepalese 10-day Vipassana Buddhist meditation[22] retreat (Dhamma Shringa), located in the foothills of the Himalayas just outside of Kathmandu. This was where I was headed. It turned out that my trek would also last 10 days—to the base

---

[21] https://en.wikipedia.org/wiki/Dalai_Lama

[22] http://www.dhamma.org.au/

of Mt Machapuchare[23] (also known as the Fishtail Mountain). Ten days of physical trekking balanced with ten days of spiritual trekking. Perfect, I thought. Being able to afford the trip to Nepal was like the most delicious icing ever on my cake of abundance.

I found the Himalayan trek to be arduous but exhilarating. Along the way, our group stayed in lodges where we were looked after by cheerful and caring Nepalese hosts. There was only one drawback for me, which was that our group comprised two Christian missionaries who were very adamant in sharing their faith. I judged this to be the height of arrogance as I did not feel they respected the Hindu and Buddhist beliefs of our Nepalese hosts. When I shared my New Age beliefs, I felt very condemned by these missionaries. After a particularly upsetting confrontation, I avoided speaking to them for the remainder of our trek. Because of this discomfort, I was relieved to finish it and eager to begin the Vipassana Buddhist silent meditation retreat.

Vipassana, which means to see things as they really are, is one of India's most ancient techniques of meditation, being discovered by Guatama Buddha[24] more than 2500 years ago. It aims for the total eradication of mental impurities and focuses on the deep interconnection between mind and body—self-transformation through self-observation[25]. Learning how to meditate silently on my breath seemed to be a natural progression from the mantra meditation that I had learned with Siddha Yoga ten years earlier.

---

[23] http://www.anothermag.com/design-living/8893/the-untouched-holy-mountain-of-nepal

[24] https://www.britannica.com/biography/Buddha-founder-of-Buddhism

[25] https://tricycle.org/magazine/vipassana-meditation/ Accessed August 2018

We were encouraged to meditate silently on the breath for one-hour morning and night. Meditation on loving kindness[26] was also encouraged. During this retreat I experienced lucid dreams, seeing spirits so clearly that they would appear to be as real people. I got very sick at one stage and some of these spirits would harass me until I told them sternly to go away. After a few days, I recovered and went on to have an especially profound experience during one meditation. My physical body appeared as a collection of cells vibrating and pulsating. I could even see the membranes joining the cells together. I felt as though I was limitless; a part of space and time beyond this physical realm.

During these times of deep meditation, it also became very clear to me what I wanted most of all in my life—that is to find "the one" and have a baby. Less than two months after my return from Nepal I met the man who I believed fit the bill.

It was love at first sight! I laid eyes on this handsome man and boom! I felt like I had been struck by lightning, electricity, fireworks—the lot. I had never felt it before or since. I believed that because I had gotten so clear about what I wanted for my life, I would now automatically attract the man of my dreams. The type of man who was close to being "realised" like me. The man who was perfect for me. The man who was my true love—my soulmate.

Things moved very quickly. I have since learned that this can be one of the hallmarks of abusive relationships—things moving too fast in a pressuring way, with little time to get to know each other properly first. Within a month this man and I had moved in together. Two months later, I was pregnant with our first daughter.

---

[26] Lovingkindness is also mentioned in Scripture – for example, *Nehemiah 9:17*; *Psalms 17:7, 31:21, 36:7, 63:3, 69:16* and *117:2*; *Isaiah 54:8* and *63:7*

FROM NEW AGE TO NEW CREATION

At first, this man was a very attentive partner, wanting to be with me all the time and seeming to be caring and thoughtful. However, he wasn't too keen on mixing with my wide circle of friends and so mostly, it was just the two of us. Slowly but surely, he began to isolate me from my friends. Derogatory comments about my appearance or personality began to be made. I tried to ignore them and brush them off but they made me feel nervous and unsettled. There were many aspects of my life where his behaviour was very controlling—for instance, he would try to dictate to me what I could buy or what social occasions I would attend. Most of my friends were worried about me, warning me that this relationship was not healthy. I, however, was not listening.

In my heart, I knew what my friends were saying was true. However, my mind was already in the process of being trapped and crippled by fear. Soon, I was totally trapped by this man. I had no knowledge or experience of how to cope with this, and I felt powerless to stop it. The charming and wonderful man of my dreams had now revealed himself to be the manipulative and abusive man of my worst nightmares.

CHAPTER 4

Into My Heart

*2 **Corinthians** 5:17 Therefore, if anyone is in Christ, he is a new creation; old things have passed away; behold, all things have become **new**.*

***Romans** 5:5 Now hope does not disappoint, because the **love** of God has been poured out in our hearts by the Holy Spirit who was given to us. 6 For when we were still without strength, in due time Christ died for the ungodly.*

I call the years of my marriage the wilderness years. Much like the Israelites wandering in the desert, I kept on in that desolate place, hoping one day to reach my Promised Land of living happily ever. The Israelites wandered for 40 years, complaining and whining, on a journey that should have taken only 11 days. But God loved them, taught them and never stopped providing for them—with manna, water, quails and spiritual guidance (*Exodus, Chapter 16*).

God eventually delivered only two of that generation, Joshua and Caleb, into the Promised Land of milk and honey. He fulfilled His promise. When my time was right, I too was able to cross over into my Promised Land of freedom and abundance. Like the Israelites, my journey was a lengthy one. Not 40 years—but, at 20, a sizeable chunk of time. Like the Israelites, I often complained and whined—but secretly, inside my mind. Like the Israelites, God cared for me, taught me and provided for me.

Amidst the turmoil and violence of that time, I believe God looked after me and, on many occasions, kept me from dying.

Having never experienced domestic violence with an intimate partner before, it came as a huge shock the first time I got hit. This happened very soon after I fell pregnant with our first child. This should have been a time when I was being cared for and nurtured, allowing the baby inside me to grow in safety and security. Not only was I suffering but so was this tiny defenceless baby—this new life who deserved nothing but love and nurturing. I found it impossible to accept that a man was capable of abusing his own wife and child. Not only was I in a state of shock but I was also in a state of denial. I just could not wrap my mind around the fact that I was getting hit, especially since it had only started when I fell pregnant.

Soon the verbal, physical and emotional abuse became regular. I fled two or three times and at one stage I tried to back out of the upcoming marriage. Threatened with death, I went ahead and married my abuser, believing that things would change for the better once we were man and wife.

It is painful to recount events of the marriage and how I, who had done so much "work" on myself, could attract an abusive narcissist. But this is exactly what happened. During the marriage, I became a shell of my former self. I who had been so independent and successful at my business, helping and empowering people, now became dependent, helpless and completely disempowered. I felt like a total fool and blamed myself for not being pretty enough or strong enough—for simply not being enough. It seems crazy to me now that I should think this way. But this reflected the crazy—and very dangerous—situation I found myself in.

Shortly after the marriage, when I was six months pregnant, I fled yet again after another abusive episode. This time I went to my parents to have my baby in peace and safety. Not long after she was born I reconciled with my husband. He had found business premises and started to work as a Bowen Therapist, which he was very skilled at. He had stopped using drugs. We had a lovely home in the country and, with our new baby, were in the "honeymoon phase" of our reconciliation. The inevitable cracks started to appear when my husband decided we would leave our home after a dispute with the real estate we were renting from.

With very little money and nowhere to live, we alternated between living with friends, on our business premises and eventually in our Kombi van. I still had all my massage clients and so I joined forces with my husband in the business. This was a hugely stressful time trying to juggle the demands of being a new mother and working, with no secure home base. There was a lot of fighting as my husband chose to pour all of our money into the business instead of finding us a new home. He was also back to feeding his drug habit.

Our growing baby was not developing normally in this very unhealthy environment. She was not reaching her developmental milestones and had a turned eye. I suffered postnatal depression, compounded by the regular physical and verbal abuse. Once again, I felt forced to flee. Following the pattern that had begun to be established, this separation was short-lived, and I went back to my husband. I believed his tearful pleas that he had changed. I believed him when he told me he loved me and our child and that he wanted to be a family.

He decided we would quit our business and try a fresh start in Queensland, where he had lived much of his childhood. Travelling and living in our Kombi van, we got as far as New South Wales before the inevitable abuse got too much for me and once again, I fled with our daughter. This time, I lived in a refuge and I started to get my life back on track. I was given support and assistance to achieve the goal of moving into my own home. I wanted to get a divorce but because my husband and I had not yet been married a year we had to undertake court-ordered counselling. Once again, we reconciled as I was drawn back into the web of his lies.

I realise now that this was a pattern of domestic violence and that there is a predictable cycle of abuse. I also realise now that my husband was a narcissist[27] and a compulsive liar. He was actually incapable of safe and healthy love. But at that time, I had no idea about narcissistic abuse[28] and I believed his lies that he could change. He had quit his consistent drug abuse and I believed that he could stick to being drug-free. Because I believed his abusive behaviour was due to his drug abuse, his being drug-free would therefore logically lead to the abuse permanently stopping. My beliefs proved faulty.

When our daughter was around 18 months old, we found a house to live in and I fell pregnant with our second daughter. Our elder daughter was still not developing normally. She had said very few words over the course of her young life and it was obvious that there was something very wrong. She was subsequently diagnosed with intellectual impairment and global developmental delay.

We were able to begin early intervention in the hope that we could address some of these delays. This was cut short as, having fallen back into his drug habits and making some enemies over money that he owed, my husband left us with no choice but to once again move. And quickly. Virtually overnight, we packed up and were on the road once again. Our new daughter was just two months old.

---

[27] https://www.psychologytoday.com/au/conditions/narcissistic-personality-disorder

[28] https://pro.psychcentral.com/exhausted-woman/2015/05/the-narcissistic-cycle-of-abuse/ All accessed August 2018

FROM NEW AGE TO NEW CREATION

This time, we made it to Queensland and entered into a relatively stable period in our marriage. My husband's behaviour and habits were still very erratic at times, but my two girls gave me a different focus and I loved being a Mum. I was also a stepmother to three other girls from my husband's first marriage. I was able to build a relationship with them as they had begun to reconnect with their father.

My children and stepchildren were *"the road in the wilderness and rivers in the desert"* (*Isaiah 43:18*). My older daughter by this time had lost all her speech so we recommenced early intervention and had her squint surgically corrected. My younger daughter's development was normal. She was a beautiful and contented baby. My husband would do occasional Bowen treatments and also went into partnership with one of his mates in a boat yard. We taught therapeutic massage courses and I would do occasional tarot card readings and channellings. I concentrated on bringing my daughters up as best I could, in the environment that we were in.

When the girls were two and four, I received the news that my father was very ill and so we packed up and moved from Queensland to Victoria to be with him. I spent six months visiting him in hospital and will always be grateful for this time. After he passed away, we moved to Tasmania for yet another "fresh start", further abuse and, predictably, yet another separation. During this separation, I went back to University, studying to be an Early Childhood teacher. Predictably, yet another reconciliation occurred. Then my husband injured his back quite badly and underwent an operation. His sister passed away at this time and as a result, my husband began to re-establish phone contact with his parents, from whom he had been estranged for many years. I would have phone conversations with his mother—a Jehovah's Witness—about religion and faith and God.

My father-in-law also became quite ill at this time and so we moved back to Queensland to be closer to him. I remember thinking that I might find religion and a faith in God through my mother-in-law. Sure enough, I *did* find this—but certainly not in the way I expected.

I was determined to find work when we moved. In 2007, I began working as a support worker at a group home for adults with disabilities. The following year I secured a job as a Kindergarten teacher. It was here that one of the teachers, a born-again Christian, began witnessing to me about Jesus. She talked to me about having a relationship with Jesus, saying this was different from having religious beliefs *about* Him. I liked our conversations. They were not like the ones I had with my mother-in-law about Jehovah, where I got the impression that you had to be a certain way—or else you would be condemned. That didn't attract me at all. But the idea of Jesus did. The grace and forgiveness He offered did. He was drawing me closer.

In 2009 my life was thrown into turmoil once again when my Mum was diagnosed with small cell lung cancer. Tragically—or perhaps mercifully—she succumbed quickly to this illness, passing away after only four months. This time, because of my job and because the girls were settled in school, we did not move to be near her. I was, however, able to attend her funeral. I don't know for sure whether Mum had a faith in Jesus but her funeral service would seem to indicate she did. My godmother, one of Mum's best friends, was a Christian, so perhaps Mum was too. The priest who was officiating at her funeral seemed very friendly and approachable. I remember thinking that if there was a priest like him where I lived, I would like to go to his church.

When I came back home after the funeral I spoke regularly with my teacher friend about Jesus and His message of forgiveness and acceptance, freedom and salvation. We spoke about how it was possible to have a personal relationship with Him. My friend would pray for me and with me. My New Age beliefs were little help to me in soothing the grief over losing my mother. They seemed to now be a surface thing instead of a foundational anchor for whatever circumstances I found myself in. I so badly wanted a change in my life. I already believed in God and, because of my conversations with my teacher friend, I wanted to believe in and know Jesus.

I wanted to know this Jesus who died an agonising death on a Cross as he took on all humankind's past, present and future sin. I wanted to know this Jesus, who through His grace and mercy, provided a way for all people to be forgiven of all their sins—to make a fresh start in their lives by accepting Him and forming a personal relationship with Him. I wanted to know this Jesus who, when we accept Him, gives us life eternal with God in Heaven. I wanted to know this Jesus who is the way, the truth and the life[29]—and the only way to God, our Heavenly Father. I wanted to know this Jesus who, after His death on that Cross, rose again three days later. I wanted to know this Jesus who will one day return to restore peace and order to this lost and hurting world that we live in.

I wanted Jesus! A *relationship* with Jesus. It was that simple. It wasn't rituals, wearing Sunday best and sitting in a pew listening to somebody preach about a distant God. It wasn't looking down my nose thinking I was perfect, and others weren't because I had Jesus in my life and they didn't. It wasn't a doctrine or set of beliefs I had to stringently keep. It was a *relationship* with Jesus—a commitment to Him and to His ways—and later, a *revelation* of who He is and what He did for me—and for all of humankind.

My opportunity came when, one afternoon in March of 2010, my friend asked me to come to her house after work for a cup of tea. There was

---

[29] *John 14.6 Jesus answered, "I am the way, the truth and the life. No one comes to the Father except through Me."*

no reason why I should feel scared—but I did. I actually felt way more than just scared. I felt totally fearful—but I went anyway. My friend and I talked about sin and what that meant (a well-rounded definition of sin is offered in the footnotes[30]). The thought that I could be a sinner seemed so radical and removed from who I believed myself to be. It made me feel decidedly uncomfortable! I believed myself to be a good person who had tried to live a good life. I didn't break the law. I tried to be kind and helpful to others. I loved my girls and cared for my husband as best I could. I took my job as a Kindergarten teacher seriously and I felt very responsible for nurturing those little lives in my charge. How could I be a sinner? It seemed so harsh!

In reality, though, I could not describe myself as someone who had never done anything wrong. I had done so much wrong! I had actually committed nearly every sin mentioned in the Bible. If I was being honest with myself—*really* honest with myself—then I had to accept the fact that I *was* (very) sinful and selfish (*Romans 3:10 As it is written: "There is none righteous, no, not one*). But this was only half the equation.

The other half of the equation to admitting that I was sinful and selfish was the fact that Jesus did not condemn me for this. The Bible teaches there is no condemnation in Christ Jesus (*Romans 8:1 There is therefore now no condemnation to those who are in Christ Jesus, who do not walk according to the flesh, but according to the Spirit*). There is no condemnation when we accept Jesus and begin to "walk in the spirit". We are all of us equally lost— whether we define ourselves as "good" people or "bad" people—before

---

[30] https://www.ucg.org/the-good-news/how-does-the-bible-define-sin Accessed August 2018

we accept Jesus. It is impossible for us to save ourselves—only He can save us[31].

So, with a simple prayer, I invited Jesus to come into my heart—and I entered into His. I allowed Him to find me; I allowed Him to fill up the "God-shaped hole" that Blaise Pascal speaks of in his book *Pensees*[32]. St Augustine of Hippo in his *Confessions*[33] wrote: "*You have made us for yourself, O Lord, and our hearts are restless until they rest in you.*" The love of God is "agape" love, the type of love which always seeks the highest good of the other person. It is the unconditional love God has for the world.

I don't remember exactly what was said when my friend and I prayed. It was generally about saying sorry to God for being a sinner, asking Jesus into my heart and starting a new life living His way. The importance of praying aloud to ask Jesus into our hearts is stated in *Romans 10:9 that if you confess with your mouth the Lord Jesus and* **believe** *in your heart that God has raised Him from the dead, you will be saved.* I didn't feel much different after we prayed, except that all that fear I had been experiencing had disappeared.

Despite the fear disappearing, I wasn't sure if Jesus really had come into my heart. It seemed so simple—*too* simple? So, I asked God for a sign that He was real. When I got home that afternoon I said to my younger daughter "Guess what happened to me today?" to which she replied, "Well, guess what happened to me today?" As it turned out, her school

---

[31] *Romans 10:3 For they being ignorant of God's righteousness, and seeking to establish their own righteousness, have not submitted to the righteousness of God. 4 For Christ is the end of the law for righteousness to everyone who believes.*

[32] https://www.enotes.com/topics/pensees

[33] https://en.wikipedia.org/wiki/Confessions_(Augustine) Both accessed August 2018

had been visited by some people from the Gideons Bible Society and she had said the prayer for salvation that was in the back of the little bible they had given her. We had both accepted Jesus at roughly the same time!

I think it was safe to say I had gotten my sign.

I asked my friend what I should do next. She advised me to speak with Jesus as though *He* was my friend—just as you would do in the beginning of any meaningful relationship. Even though it took a bit of getting used to, I began to speak with Jesus regularly and this helped build a relationship with Him. My friend also advised me to find a church to attend. The father of one of my Kindergarten children happened to be the pastor of a small church. I didn't think my husband would allow me to attend church on a Sunday. Instead, on Friday afternoons (without my husband's knowledge) my younger daughter and I began attending a course called "Introducing God" with the pastor and his wife at their house. This course gave us a foundation for our new faith and, with many stops and starts, took about a year to complete.

One of the things that stood out clearly to me during this time was the love and grace extended to me and my daughter by this young couple. They never pressured me about how long it was taking to finish the course. We worked through it at our own pace. Another thing that stood out was when the pastor spoke about Jesus dying and rising again. This was something no other prophet or religious figure—not Buddha[34], Mohammad[35], Confucius[36], Lao-Tze[37] or anyone else—had ever done.

---

[34] https://thebuddhistcentre.com/text/who-was-buddha

[35] https://en.wikipedia.org/wiki/Muhammad

[36] https://en.wikipedia.org/wiki/Confucius

[37] https://en.wikipedia.org/wiki/Laozi All accessed August 2018

FROM NEW AGE TO NEW CREATION

The fact that Jesus overcame death was a huge eye-opener for me. Who *was* this Jesus? And how could He overcome death?

That first year of talking with Jesus was mostly spent asking Him to fix my marriage or make me into the wife my husband needed. My husband had already made known his displeasure with religion, so I felt I had to hide the fact that I had accepted Jesus and became born again. I hoped that Jesus would heal my pain! I would walk on the beach each morning, talking with Him and praying about what I wanted in my marriage. I loved communing with Jesus in the splendour of nature. This has never changed. I feel very close to my Creator when I am in His creation.

Looking back at this time I can see that I wanted my marriage to be healthy. I wanted to love my husband and to be able to trust him. The reality of the situation was that all the emotional healing I had undertaken during my time in the New Age had not prevented me from experiencing the devastation of a marriage with a narcissistic drug-addicted partner who was incapable of giving and receiving a healthy and safe love.

And maybe I was incapable of love myself? I did not love my husband. At times I absolutely hated him. When confronted with the intense pain of the abusive marriage, on some level I believed it was my fault. I believed if I were prettier, or thinner, or understood him better, my husband would not hurt me. On another level, I was in denial about just how bad the abuse was. And on yet another level, a part of me realised that I did NOT deserve the abusive treatment, that it was just plain wrong. Before I found out that narcissists existed and what narcissism was, my reasoning as to why I had attracted a violent partner was because I had unaddressed childhood experiences. I believed these childhood experiences had built up a negative belief system about who I was and what I deserved. If I could replace this with a positive belief system I could turn this situation around. Now I realise that this was faulty and unwise thinking. I was in danger and in complete denial about how unsafe my situation was.

One of my brothers was quite physically and emotionally abusive towards me during my early teenage years. During this time, I had also experienced physical abuse from two boys in my class. I had been very close to one of these boys throughout my childhood, so this treatment was really tough on me. Because of this, I believe I built up a pattern of accepting violent behaviour in close relationships. Even though, as an adult I had experienced loving relationships with decent men, these relationships invariably ended with them leaving. Abandonment was pretty entrenched within me. An abusive husband would never leave me. He was too busy controlling me. This is what I did not want to accept.

My marriage was a journey into deep, dark, intense pain. I was locked for over 20 years in a cycle of abuse where I would leave and then go back after a while because my husband would track me down, cry and say he was sorry. He would tell me he had changed and that he couldn't live without me. He would beg us to be a family again. It was relentless. He wore me down every single time. Each time I believed my husband when he said he would change.

I simply did not realise what I was up against. Severe and debilitating pain was how I would describe my marriage. The pain of the emptiness of being married to someone who cannot be trusted. The pain of realising I was trapped in a cycle of abuse. The desolate pain that came as I surrendered the idea that I had a purpose and meaning for my life. Self-worth and dignity were buried beneath the layers of abuse that I had accepted for so long. I did not believe that I could ever break free. I was sick and tired of leaving my husband and reconciling with him. I resigned myself to accepting that it was my "fate" to stay in this unhealthy marriage. I had become a victim in every sense of the word.

FROM NEW AGE TO NEW CREATION

But resigning myself to a marriage that is like a living death is not what God teaches in His Scriptures. In early March of 2011, I was hit for the final time. This was the culmination of a day of my husband drinking and mixing various painkillers. Without going into too much detail, let it be said that there were many unspeakably horrifying twists and turns on that night. I feared for my life and was deeply anguished over what my children, then young teenagers, were witnessing. On that night, though, God's might was revealed as I heard His voice and experienced His power in a way I had never known before.

It wasn't the still, small voice I was accustomed to hearing. This time, God's voice was loud and clear. I will never forget the words that allowed me to begin, in His authority, to be free of my abusive marriage once and for all.

"THIS . . . STOPS . . . NOW!"

Time seemed to slow down and stand still as I saw this man—my husband—out of his mind on alcohol and drugs, seemingly fly across the room towards me and punch me full on in the face. As my face exploded, my survival mechanism kicked in. I fled—across the road to a neighbour's house. My husband fled also—in our car—but was apprehended by the police and taken into custody. My girls and I were taken to a motel for the night where we would be safe. We had taken our first steps to freedom. This time, the freedom would last.

As a child of God, I was finally able to break free once and for all of the entanglement and entrapment of my marriage. Although it would take four more years before I was officially divorced, that night God saved me and set me on the road to freedom from my hellish marriage. I do not doubt for one second that it was God's voice I heard. It was His voice that finally broke the chains of illusion that had bound me.

Despite praying to God many times to help me be the wife my husband needed, in the end, God did not keep me in this marriage. He delivered me from it. He delivered me from the husband and father who had never protected nor provided for his family. And God did it in His perfect time.

I knew that Satan—the enemy—was real that night as I saw my husband appear to fly across the room towards me, towering over me with his eyes as black as the dead of night. I believe he was demon possessed and that these demons[38] had entered through the doorway of drug and alcohol abuse. Once before, in the 1980s, I had a bad magic mushroom trip and I experienced the enemy in the room with me, laughing at me and tormenting me. I had prayed to God to save me that night, holding onto Him for dear life until morning came, and the enemy vanished. This time, as I experienced demonic attack through my crazed husband, I held onto God for dear life again.

Looking back—not just at these times but at other times during my life—I believe my heart knew I belonged to God long before my mind did. For example, back in August 1987, at a time when my journal contained very detailed reflections on what was happening in my life, one entry stands out as a stark contrast to the usual things I would write about. It was like an oasis in a desert—cool and refreshing.

---

[38] A demon is a fallen angel. When Satan, who was the very highest angel, rebelled against God, he took a large number of the angels with him in rebellion (*Isaiah 14:12-15* and *Revelation 12:3-4*). When their rebellion failed, they were cast out of Heaven. Those angels are now demons. As angels can ascend the heights of spirituality, demons reach the depths of hatred, bitterness, and perversion. Demons torment and harass people, leading them away from God and His truth (*Mark 5:2-5, Acts 13:6-12*). Excerpt from What is a Demon? Kingdom Dynamics, New Spirit Filled Life Bible, p. 1357.

FROM NEW AGE TO NEW CREATION

"I would not turn the clock back for anything. So I thank God and praise Him for granting me the path I now tread. I am thankful I am what I am and where I am." The only way that I can explain this entry is that I believe God was present and working on my heart, laying the groundwork for what was to come. Although at the time my mind was fully immersed in New Age philosophy and I paid God scant attention, I obviously felt such gratitude that He was there. Looking back now, I believe He was drawing me to Him, ready to meet me when the time was right.

In Ecclesiastes 3:11 we find *"He has made everything beautiful in its time. Also, He has put eternity in their hearts, except that no one can find out the work that God does from beginning to end."* To me, the love of God, who sent Jesus, is a mystery. I get glimpses of how much He loves me. When I was at my lowest ebb, I know He was there as a tiny stirring of hope. He was a voice that whispered to my heart—not so much with words but with the impression of His magnificent love—(*Matthew 11:28 "Come to Me, all you who labour and are heavy laden, and I will give you rest."*)

In hindsight, I can see God's fingerprints all over my life, sustaining me, protecting me and setting me apart. I should have died numerous times. As for my marriage, it was not until I accepted Jesus Christ and finally got saved that I was given the strength to leave the abusive union *permanently* and *never* go back. You see, getting saved and starting to journey alongside the Creator of the Universe gave me some pretty handy hints about what love was. And about what was love was not.

The love of Jesus is unlike any other. As mentioned earlier in this chapter, it is the only perfect example of love, known as agape love. His love, His goodness, His grace, His mercy, His forgiveness and His promises are all demonstrated and recorded through Scripture. Because He is perfectly trustworthy, I can believe the Scriptures when they tell me the way He thinks about me (for example, *Jeremiah 29:11 For I know the thoughts that I think toward you, says the LORD, thoughts of peace and not of evil, to give you a future and a hope*). I can believe Him when He says that I am *"fearfully and wonderfully made"* (Psalm 139:14) and that He is making new things spring forth, like *"a road in the wilderness and rivers in the desert"* (Isaiah 43:19).

When I allowed Jesus to come into my heart, all of the issues which had brought me to the point of no return in the marriage began to be addressed by His loving presence. In His perfect time, the process was beginning to transform my life at its deepest level.

CHAPTER 5

Building Faith

Hebrews 11:1 *Now faith is the substance of things hoped for, the evidence of things not seen. 2 For by it the elders obtained a good testimony. 3 By faith we understand that the worlds were framed by the word of God, so that the things which are seen were not made of things which are visible.*

Hebrews 11:6 *But without faith it is impossible to please Him, for he who comes to God must believe that He is, and that He is a rewarder of those who diligently seek Him.*

I had received my answer from God regarding my marriage. The answer was that it was over. Days after being hit and going to a women's refuge, Cyclone Yasi also hit, devastating our region and causing widespread flooding. It was a couple of weeks before I could go back to my old house to collect my belongings (with police protection).

In the midst of packing up my things, I felt the Lord clearly impress upon me to throw out all my New Age books and oracles. There were so many of these that I had loved and used regularly—yet letting go of them was an easy process because it was so clear that this was what the Lord required me to do. Jesus was liberating me from everything that was not for my good.

I was blessed to be able to rent the house of my pastor and his wife, who had relocated to the country. I became very involved with my church. This church was not like the very regimented church of my childhood. My new church felt much more relaxed, with scriptural teaching that had practical application for my life. There was a real and authentic connection with others. It was joyful!

My faith continued to grow and the growth that I was experiencing in my relationship with Jesus led to me getting baptised in 2011. I never thought I would be the type of person to get baptised, because I never thought that my relationship with Jesus would mean that much to me! My faith in Jesus and my growing relationship with Him made it so that baptism became the natural next step. Besides talking with Jesus, praying and attending church regularly, I also read a lot of Christian fiction, including Frank E. Peretti's *"This Present Darkness"*[39] and the *"Left Behind"*[40] series of books by Tim LaHaye and Jerry Jenkins. When I was at home, I had Vision Christian Radio on, listening to teachings from Greg Laurie[41], Dr Chuck Missler[42], Ravi Zacharias[43] and Dr Charles Stanley[44]. Scripture teaches that faith is built by hearing (*Romans 10:17 Consequently, faith comes from hearing the message, and the message is heard through the word about Christ*).

By listening to these messages, I was indeed building my faith in Jesus. Consistently, I was doing those things which grew my relationship with Him.

---

[39] https://en.wikipedia.org/wiki/This_Present_Darkness

[40] https://en.wikipedia.org/wiki/Left_Behind

[41] https://www.harvest.org/watch-and-listen/radio

[42] https://www.khouse.org

[43] https://rzim.org

[44] https://www.intouch.org All accessed August 2018

FROM NEW AGE TO NEW CREATION

All of this contributed to a growing realisation that I also needed to read my Bible consistently. I did not do this very much in the early days of my relationship with Jesus. I recall it was a couple of years in, around 2012, when I intentionally began to read a chapter of Scripture every day. I liked to read it out loud. This progressed to reading two chapters a day—one in the morning and one at night. I actually began to hunger for the word of God. The people in the Bible started to become real for me. These were people of faith, many of whom could be termed dysfunctional (some with a capital "D"), with major issues in their lives. They were imperfect people who a perfect God used mightily to do what He needed them to do. (And if you would like to read a great article about these "messed up bible heroes", I recommend you check out footnote[45]).

These were the things that I did as I journeyed with Jesus. Another very important part of my journey was that I was blessed to be part of a small group of strong Christian women who helped me understand what it meant to be a follower of Jesus. We shared what was happening in our lives and prayed with and for each other. In this safe environment, I was able to grow in Jesus and start the process of healing from a lot of the emotional hurt and shame that I carried from the marriage. I realised my sense of self-worth and ability to trust had been much damaged. I also realised I was a chronic people pleaser who found it virtually impossible to say "no".

Intrinsic to this healing was being able to access a skilled Christian counsellor. I found Christian counselling to be a process, unlike anything I had experienced with secular counselling. I am in no way minimising the good, productive work a skilled and empathetic secular counsellor can do. As you are aware from earlier parts of this story, I did

---

[45] https://www.ministryexploit.com/20-messed-up-bible-heroes-and-what-we-can-learn-from-them

experience great personal growth through this type of counselling. In my experience though, this pales in comparison to the growth and healing that occurred within me with Christian counselling.

With the assistance of my counsellor, I would access different memories relating to the issues I needed help with. In simple terms, the process that occurred for me was that the Lord Jesus, who lives outside of time, would help me access and heal deep-seated issues. The **root cause**, where the memory originated, was identified and transformed by the Lord Jesus. The change, in my experience, was profound and *permanent*. I found healing through the power of Jesus to be a refreshing change. It was very organic, meaning it occurred naturally, at my pace. Yet it was not accomplished by natural means alone but by the supernatural touch of our powerful Creator.

Applying the blood of Jesus to cleanse and heal situations is also a very powerful transformational tool. During the first few years of my relationship with Jesus, I was uncomfortable with the idea of His blood being so powerful and transforming. How could blood transform anything? Yet as I learned to communicate and lean into Him more and began to develop the mind of Christ, this idea became less confronting. Put simply, His blood is not like ours. The sacrificial blood of Christ is the agency for cleansing, forgiveness, and redemption. It washes all our sins clean like the purest of rainwater (*1 John 1:7 But if we walk in the light as He is in the light, we have fellowship with one another, and the blood of Jesus his Son cleanses us from all sin*).

I look at entering into a relationship with Jesus as being twofold—saved by grace but also with soul issues that need to be healed by the ultimate doctor. Jesus saves us, giving us a new spirit, and then heals the wounds and hurts of our souls. This is an ongoing process; a work in progress. I am a work in progress! I choose to be willing to journey with Jesus, which means I consistently seek His guidance and counsel in all areas of my life, especially through prayer. This is so that I may be freed up to step more fully into the plan He has for my (and every) life. I do my best to apply what He teaches, taking the necessary steps of action to accomplish this. This is always a choice and not often an easy one. I get very easily distracted and I often feel overwhelmed with, and unable to cope with, what is happening in my life.

This is where my relationship with Jesus is so precious. Instead of having a perspective that there is something wrong with me because I don't have everything together, I now find, through my life in Jesus, that I have been given a different, fresh perspective. This perspective is that needing Him as much as I do is exactly as it should be. I am loved just as I am, and I desperately need Jesus to carry me through.

I am *allowed* to not cope; I am *permitted* to be weak; it is *okay* that I don't have to try to fix things or do everything in my own strength. This is explained so well by the apostle Paul, who repeatedly grappled with a "thorn in his flesh[46]", in *2 Corinthians 12:9 And He said to me, "My grace is sufficient for you, for My strength is made perfect in weakness". Therefore most gladly I will rather boast in my infirmities, that the power of Christ may rest upon me. 10 Therefore I take pleasure in infirmities, in reproaches, in needs, in persecutions, in distresses, for Christ's sake. For when I am weak, then I am strong.*

I know that Jesus's strength is infinite and that He is perfectly equipped to be strong for me. I can allow the Creator of the Universe to lift me up into His strength, as taught in *Philippians 4:13 I can do all things through Christ who strengthens me.* I can relax! I am loved! Not because I have it all together but because I am His. He takes care of me so beautifully.

It is because I am His that I can also rest easy that He is always there for me in my time of need. There are many Scriptures which teach this. A

---

[46] *2 Corinthians 12:7 Therefore, in order to keep me from becoming conceited, I was given a thorn in my flesh, a messenger of Satan, to torment me.*

great one is *Hebrews 4:16 Let us therefore come boldly to the throne of grace, that we may obtain mercy and find grace to help in time of need.*

It has been hard for me to admit my weakness and my frailty because I have been so used to being strong. Within the turmoil of my marriage and caring for my children, especially my elder daughter with her challenging behaviours, I have had to be strong. Yet each time something challenging or difficult would occur and I chose to lean into Jesus He brought me through every single time.

An example of this occurred in October of 2015. The organisation that had been supporting my daughter was no longer prepared to do this. My daughter's challenging behaviours were becoming increasingly violent. The organisation wanted her medicated, but this was not as simple as it sounds. In the past, there had been very troubling side-effects from anti-depressant or anti-psychotic medications. I did not believe this was a suitable course of action for my daughter.

I would have to find an alternative means of support for her. We would need to move to the nearest city to access suitable services, in order to help manage my daughter's many challenges. This in itself was a hugely daunting task. There was also the problem of having a term left of my Kindergarten teaching year. I did not want to abandon this responsibility if I could possibly avoid it.

When it became evident that we would have to move, I cried solidly on and off for two days, not knowing what to do and where to turn. To say I felt completely overwhelmed by the situation would be an understatement. Amidst my emotional turmoil and sobbing to God, I could just make out His still, small voice. He kept whispering to my heart, over and over, *"Be still and know that I am God" (Psalm 46:10)* and *Proverbs 3:5 "Trust in the LORD with all your heart, And lean not on your own understanding; 6 In all your ways acknowledge Him and He shall direct your paths."* These whispers to my heart and mind, these nudges from the

FROM NEW AGE TO NEW CREATION

Holy Spirit, were Him reminding me that I could trust Him. They were Him reminding me that He was God and I was not. If I could choose to lean *on* Him and lean *into* Him, He would take care of me and every detail of my situation.

I was, however, so used to doing things in my own strength and so I stubbornly refused to acknowledge that He was there to take care of me. Finally, I let go and let God. I surrendered. I just could not do this in my own strength. There were so many details that needed to be attended to in order to make the move. It was simply too much for me to handle. Sure enough, God took care of them all—working through people and through miraculous interventions that were so timely and perfect there could be no doubt He was responsible.

For instance, a large sum of money was made available in a very unexpected way. Travel arrangements and suitable accommodation for my daughter fell into place. She would spend two days in respite in the city each week, which allowed me to finish off my last term of teaching. The transformational might and power of God was working through people and places, bringing all things together for the good of those who love Him (*Romans 8:28 And we know that all things work together for good to those who love God, to those who are called according to His purpose*). And oh, how I love Him! This love deepened as I allowed myself to trust God and the process He was guiding me through.

I leaned in so close to Jesus, literally clinging to Him amidst the darkness and uncertainty of that time. His presence was so close and clear that to this day it still brings tears to my eyes as I remember the care and love He lavished on me. Every single detail was taken care of over and above what I could have imagined. That is God. As I said, trusting Him and allowing Him to take charge was very difficult to do. However, once I surrendered, God's provision was outstanding. The way opened up easily as we successfully transitioned into our new home and the next chapter of our lives.

CHAPTER 6

Resting in God's Promises

Psalm 56:8 *You number my wanderings;*
Put my tears into Your bottle;
Are they not in Your book?
9 When I cry out to You,
Then my enemies will turn back;
This I know, because God is for me.

Psalm 23 *The Lord is my shepherd;*
I shall not want.
2 He makes me to lie down in green pastures;
He leads me beside the still waters.
3 He restores my soul;
He leads me in the paths of righteousness
For His name's sake.
4 Yea, though I walk through the valley of the shadow of death,
I will fear no evil;
For You are with me;
Your rod and Your staff, they comfort me.
5 You prepare a table before me in the presence of my enemies;
You anoint my head with oil;
My cup runs over.
6 Surely goodness and mercy shall follow me
All the days of my life;
And I will dwell in the house of the LORD
Forever.

> ***Hebrews 4:12*** *For the word of God is living and powerful, and sharper than any two-edged sword, piercing even to the division of soul and spirit, and of joints and marrow, and is a discerner of the thoughts and intents of the heart. 13 And there is no creature hidden from His sight, but all things are naked and open to the eyes of Him to whom we must give account.*

One of the underlying themes for my life was that I often felt as though I was never good enough. I often felt as though I was lacking in something essential. It was not okay to be me and so I was on a perpetual quest to heal what was "wrong" within me. Dealing with my "stuff" was ongoing and each time I had a treatment or some counselling I did feel as though I had made some progress. On the other hand, I also felt that I needed so much healing that it was like a bottomless pit.

My focus was on forgiving myself so that I would feel okay about myself. Yet so often this seemed like an impossible task because I could not forgive myself *fully* until I had healed "my stuff". I was fighting a losing battle with myself. How could I attain this elusive perfection of being fully healed? Which book should I read? Which self-help course should I do? Which treatment did I need? It was relentless.

In my experience, being born again in Jesus has been polar opposite to this. There is no more relentless striving. I can rest in Him. I—and you—don't have to do anything to **earn** Jesus' forgiveness. It doesn't matter who we are or what we have done. We can define ourselves as "good" or "bad", but this is of no relevance as far as needing Jesus goes. The truth is that everyone needs Jesus—whether we realise this or not. When we admit we need Him and accept His free gift of salvation, genuinely repenting of our sins and wanting a new life in Him, we are forgiven and set free. We are forgiven and set free through God's grace and Jesus' monumental sacrifice at the Cross. Not only are we forgiven but our sins are remembered no more (*Hebrews 8:12 "For I will be merciful to their unrighteousness, and their sins and their lawless deeds I will remember no more"*).

What a relief to find out that I wasn't some misfit or "damaged goods" but rather I was a child of God who lived in an imperfect, fallen world. It was such a relief to find out that there was a powerful explanation as to how the fallen world had come to be that way. It has been such a revelation to hear of the powerful antidote—Jesus' sacrifice at the Cross—to the poison of the enemy's work—Adam and Eve eating of the fruit of the Tree of Knowledge of good and evil. Through the Cross, we can begin again, forgiven and redeemed, in restored relationship with God.

Jesus' forgiveness means I am far more able and willing to forgive others. John Mellor in his excellent book *"Keys to Healing"*[47] speaks about the connection between un-forgiveness and healing. As John says, and what I have learned, is that forgiveness is *not* a feeling. Rather, it is a decision that is made and continues to be made each time the un-forgiveness presents itself.

Simply put, once you choose to forgive someone, you continue to keep on choosing to forgive until you can remember the original situation without pain or anger. Part of the forgiveness process is asking Jesus to bless the person who we have felt wronged by. Forgiving my ex-husband has been, and still is, an ongoing process. I made the decision to forgive because I did not wish to live in bitterness and resentment as a perpetual victim of what he did to me and our children. This does not mean I want to be anywhere in the vicinity of my ex-husband. What it does mean is that the hold he has over me and the bond of un-forgiveness is shattered. Jesus instructed us to *"Love one another as I have*

---

[47] "Keys to Healing", John Mellor (1996), Tyndale House Publishers Inc., Wheaton, Illinois, pp 142-3

loved you" *(John 15:12)* and this includes forgiveness. Nowadays, the decision to forgive also extends more easily to myself. My identity in Christ and the gift of forgiveness means I can more readily go easy on myself for all my frailties and the poor choices I have made (and still make).

Jesus' forgiveness also means that He is supremely equipped to take on what is burdening me. As you know, it has been a heavy burden for me to shoulder the endless responsibility of trying to cope with all life's hardships and challenges in my own strength. In Scripture, Jesus says He wants to take the burden from me. He promises I can do things in His strength[48] and that I am an overcomer in Him[49]. He promises me that He will never leave me nor forsake me[50] and that I can cast all my cares on Him[51]. God cannot lie[52] and so it follows that His promises are true.

There are so many more of God's promises besides the ones listed above[53]—all throughout Scripture. I find such power and authority in Scripture because it is God's breathed word. The circumstances and

---

[48] *Philippians 4:13 I can do all this through Him who gives me strength.*

[49] *1 John 5:4 For whatever is born of God overcomes the world. And This is the victory that has overcome the world—our faith. 54 Who is he who overcomes the world, but he who believes that Jesus is the Son of God?*

[50] *Deuteronomy 31:6 "Be strong and of good courage, do not fear nor be afraid of them; for the LORD your God, He is the One who goes with you. He will not leave you nor forsake you."*

[51] *Psalm 55:22 Cast your burden on the LORD and He shall sustain you; He shall never permit the righteous to be moved.*

[52] *Numbers 23:19 "God is not a man, that He should lie, Nor a son of man, that He should repent, Has He said, and will He not do? Or has He spoken, and will He not make it good?*

[53] https://www.biblegateway.com/resources/dictionary-of-bible-themes/5467-promises-divine Accessed August 2018

cultures of the people depicted in the Bible might in some ways be different from those of today, but their imperfections and humanity are very much the same as mine. And God doesn't change. He is the same yesterday and today and forever[54]. Each time I read Scripture I am reading God's living truth with the guidance of the Holy Spirit to reveal understanding to me. In this way, I find that the words of the Bible are living, dynamic and relevant.

In my experience, there is nothing in New Age that comes close to this personal teaching from the Creator of the Universe. There is a plethora of self-help "gurus" and motivational speakers out there, as well as many self-help therapies and, as you know, I personally have experienced many of these. I used the teachings of these people and the various therapies to try to heal my "stuff". Yet all of us, because we are imperfect and live in a fallen world, are essentially broken. All of us in our humanness (and precisely because of our humanness)—including the church, family, friends, the self-help gurus, motivational speakers, mega-popular Christian evangelists, fellow Christians and myself—have the capacity to betray and hurt each other. **Only Jesus** does not have this capacity.

Following Jesus means that, even though I am not perfect, I follow One who is. His perfection assists, and uplifts, my imperfection. I do my very best to live by His example. As a follower of Jesus, I am reassured that I have His mind[55] and am part of His body[56].

When I was in the New Age, I truly did not know what I was missing by not being a follower of Jesus, but I certainly had a sense that I was

---

[54] *Hebrews 13:8 Jesus Christ is the same yesterday, today, and forever.*

[55] *1 Corinthians 2:16 For "who has known the mind of the LORD that he may instruct Him?" But we have the mind of Christ.*

[56] *1 Corinthians 12:27 Now you are the body of Christ, and members individually.*

hungering and thirsting for something always just beyond my reach. I was trying to satisfy it with another therapy, another healing or another teacher with a new shiny object for me to look at and grasp onto. I believed I would come to a point where I would not only be satisfied and content but that I would become the master of my own destiny. I was trying to become my own god. I was deceived.

There is a stark contrast between how I viewed my own capacity to love and be loved through the lens of my own self—compared with the love I am promised and which I experience from my Creator. Those of us who are parents would say that there is no love like the love you have for your child. The Creator's love, described through Scriptures and experienced when you invite Jesus into your heart, is like that parental love but very much deeper and wider. Two of the many Scriptures that describe our Heavenly Father's love for His children are found in *1 John 3:1 Behold what manner of love the Father has bestowed on us, that we should be called children of God! Therefore the world does not know us, because it did not know Him*, and in *Psalm 36:7 How precious is your loving kindness, O God! Therefore the children of men put their trust under the shadow of Your wings.*

God is so totally in love with us that He gave His own son to die on the Cross so that we could experience a relationship with Him and a restoration of that which was broken at the Tree of Knowledge of good and evil in the Garden of Eden so long ago (*John 3:16 For God so loved the world that He gave His only begotten Son, that whoever believes in Him should not perish but have everlasting life*).

The spiritual battle for humanity's salvation is real[57]. As long as people are living an apparently good life, the idea of their eternal life and salvation may not even be something they would contemplate. Living a

---

[57] *Ephesians 6:12 For we do not wrestle against flesh and blood, but against principalities, against powers, against the rulers of the darkness of this age, against spiritual hosts of wickedness in the heavenly places.*

good life without considering that you also have an eternal life—and where that eternal life will be spent—means that the enemy has already stolen your chance for salvation away. He has killed and destroyed your opportunity to be with God—without you even realising this. And killing and destroying is what the enemy specialises in. In *John 10:10*, Jesus describes the enemy as a thief. Jesus says *"the thief does not come except to steal, and to kill, and to destroy. I have come that they may have life, and that they may have it more abundantly."* Eternal life in this context is therefore the *only* thing that matters[58].

When we die without accepting Jesus into our hearts, we are separated from God forever. Our lives are short, and death can come at any time. None of us knows when we are going to die (*James 4:14 whereas you do not know what will happen tomorrow. For what is your life? It is even a vapour that appears for a little time and then vanishes away*). Time is of the essence. Why risk the free gift of salvation by putting off the opportunity to get right with God today? Right here, right now?

As a Christian, my focus is on spending my lifetime for the glory of God—His infinite beauty and greatness of His perfections—safe in the knowledge that I will be spending my eternal life with Him[59]. The message of the gospel is to be shared because the salvation of every person is at stake. It was only when I began following Jesus that I even thought much about Eternity. And the question of what Eternity is and how it should be spent is answered completely by Jesus and His lavish love for us. As it is written in *John 13:34 "A new commandment I give to you,*

---

[58] *Romans 6:23 For the wages of sin is death, but the gift of God is eternal life in Christ Jesus our Lord.*

[59] *John 10:28 And I give them eternal life, and they shall never perish, neither shall anyone snatch them out of My hand. 29 My Father, who has given them to me, is greater than all; and no one is able to snatch them out of My Father's hand. I and My Father are one.*

that you love one another; as I have loved you, that you also love one another. 35 By this all will know that you are My disciples, if you have love for one another."

CHAPTER 7

Out of the Night and into the Light

John 8:12 *Then Jesus spoke to them again, saying, "I am the light of the world. He who follows Me shall not walk in darkness, but have the light of life."*

Romans 1:25 *who exchanged the truth of God for the lie, and worshiped and served the creature rather than the Creator, who is blessed forever. Amen.*

John 8:44 *"You are of your father the devil, and the desires of your father you want to do. He was a murderer from the beginning, and does not stand in the truth, because there is no truth in him. When he speaks a lie, he speaks from his own resources, for he is a liar and the father of it. 45 But because I tell the truth, you do not believe Me."*

When I was in the New Age, I believed I was operating from a place of love for my fellow man. I saw myself as an honourable person doing good for others. I took the responsibility of my healing work very seriously, and it was very important to me that it was carried out with the highest of integrity. The teachings of love and light that I embraced encompassed a wide number of modalities under the umbrella of the New Age. However, the monumental flaw that was inherent within my belief system was that I did not ponder nor question the foundation upon which the teachings of the New Age were built.

I was mistaken by my belief that the New Age teachings *came* from love and light. My intention was certainly loving, and the teachings certainly *appeared* to be loving. Just as planting an apple seed cannot yield pears, so too, planting a seed of deception and occult practice cannot yield love and light. While I kept thinking and believing I was in the light, I was, in reality, in the shadows. I just did not see it because I was not looking for it. It did not enter my mind to look for it.

The shadow is the place of illusion—a reflection or distortion of something real. The shadow itself is *not real* yet at the same time it is visible and apparent; in this way, it *appears* to be real. The word shadow can be defined in various ways[60] and each definition adds up to how I was unknowingly living in the shadows, as well as *being* shadowed by the enemy, who at that stage I really had no idea about. Some of the definitions of a shadow are 1. As a noun: a dark figure or image cast on the ground or some surface by a body intercepting light. 2. As a verb (used with object): to follow (a person) about secretly, in order to keep watch over his movements. 3. As an adjective: Without official authority, e.g. a shadow government.

The shadow side of each person, as taught in New Age teachings, was something which needed to be embraced in order for true healing to occur. All the pain resided within the shadow. Once a person was healed, the shadow side would then integrate with the positive side of the personality. Effectively, the shadow side would then cease to exist.

When I came to Christ, I came to realise that this shadow was, in fact, a wound. It was a spiritual wound forged at the beginning of time, with its origins in a garden. This garden was a wondrously beautiful place, in which every need of those who inhabited it was taken care of perfectly. I came to realise that this spiritual wound first occurred when the perfect

---

[60] http://www.dictionary.com/browse/shadow Accessed August 2018

relationship between Creator and His creation—man and woman—was violated.

When God created the world, it is written that He saw that it was "good", and man's creation was "very good". In the Book of Genesis, the first book in the Holy Bible, we see God as the true foundation. God is the ultimate Creator. Everything flows from Him and His Word. Man was originally created in the image of God![61] The basis of creation according to the Bible is that it is good (Chapter 1 in the *Book of Genesis*). The enemy's plan to undermine God's authority and try to become Him began with a deceptively simple question. In *Genesis 3:1* we read *Now the serpent was more cunning than any beast of the field which the LORD God had made. And he said to the woman, "Has God indeed said, 'You shall not eat of every tree of the garden'?"* The seed of doubt is planted in Eve's mind as she begins to question God's authority.

Later, we see God's authority undermined by the enemy as Eve and then Adam eat of the fruit from the Tree of knowledge of good and evil. This is recorded in *Genesis 3:4 Then the serpent said to the woman, "You will not surely die. 5 "For God knows that in the day you eat of it your eyes will be opened, and you will be like God, knowing good and evil."*

With one bite from the fruit of the Tree of knowledge of good and evil (Genesis 3:6), sin seeped into their hearts. In a place lush and ripe with abundance and harmony, this tree was the only place off limits. For the very first time, the human man and woman encountered an enemy (Satan, in the guise of a serpent) whose mission was to "kill, steal and destroy". Satan, once one of God's most loved angels called Lucifer, was

---

[61] *Genesis 1:26 Then God said, "Let Us make man in Our image, according to Our likeness; let them have dominion over the fish of the sea, over the birds of the air, and over the cattle, over all the earth and over every creeping thing that creeps on the earth." 27 So God created man in His own image; in the image of God He created him; male and female He created them.*

in love with his own beauty and fell into pride and self-centredness. So, he had been banished because he wanted to *be like* God (*Isaiah 14:12-15*)[62]. This could never be.

Instead, he is the counterfeit version of God, specialising in deception and illusion and hating God's creation with a vengeance. Evil thrives where there is deception. It flourishes where there is an enemy who is the exact opposite of a pure and loving God. The enemy has many abilities, including his ability to appear as an angel of light. The Apostle Paul tells us this in *2 Corinthians 11:13 For such are false apostles, deceitful workers, transforming themselves into apostles of Christ. 14 And no wonder! For* **Satan himself transforms himself into an angel of light**[63]. *15 Therefore it is no great thing if his ministers also transform themselves into ministers of righteousness, whose end will be according to their works.* The enemy and those who serve him—wolves in sheep's clothing—can be very skilled at *appearing* to be righteous and of Jesus, using the tools of deception and illusion.

The purpose of deception and illusion is to move people away from the truth. Any movement away from the truth, no matter how miniscule or slight, means it is no longer the truth. It's a lie. One tiny deception, just like at the beginning of the creation of the world in the Garden of Eden, can spread into massive consequences and large-scale deception. It is like a ripple in a pond caused by a small stone. That one small ripple spreads out into ever-increasing circles. The partial truths of the New

---

[62] *Isaiah 14:12 How you are fallen from heaven, O Lucifer, son of the morning! How you are cut down to the ground, You who weakened the nations! 13 For you have said in your heart: 'I will ascend into heaven, I will exalt my throne above the stars of God; I will also sit on the mount of the congregation On the farthest sides of the north; 14 I will ascend above the heights of the clouds, I will be like the Most High.' 15 Yet you shall be brought down to Sheol, To the lowest depths of the Pit . . .*

[63] Bold emphasis is mine

FROM NEW AGE TO NEW CREATION

Age of peace, love and light, reaping what you sow, and positive thinking may seem to align with Jesus' teachings. However, they are not the works of the Kingdom of Light. They are the works of the Kingdom of Darkness.

I say this because the *roots* of New Age are, to put it bluntly, evil. They are most definitely *not* of love and light. There is much research to back this up, a little of which I cite here. For instance, read up on Madame Blavatsky, founder of the Theosophical Society[64]. Do some research on Alice Bailey[65] and Aleister Crowley[66]. These people are the founders of New Age teachings and their ideas are of the occult[67]. As I said earlier, I accepted the "love and light" of New Age teachings readily and I did not stop to consider what foundation they might be built on.

The deception of New Age teachings extended to Jesus and God. The Jesus (also known as Sananda[68]) I knew through New Age teachings was most definitely *not* the Jesus of the Holy Bible. Rather, He was relegated to a position of one in a group of seven Ascended Masters[69]. Having not heard the gospel, nor read much of the Bible, I did not question this. I welcomed the New Age perspective on Jesus, thinking that the New Age had gotten it right. To me, this was another indication of how the New Age embraced all philosophies and was the epitome of tolerance and goodness. To my mind, "god and goddess—all that is" was much

---

[64] http://blavatskyarchives.com/longseal.htm

[65] https://en.wikipedia.org/wiki/Alice_Bailey

[66] http://new-age-spirituality.com/philos/crowley.html

[67] https://en.wikipedia.org/wiki/Occult

[68] http://sananda.website/sananda/

[69] https://www.summitlighthouse.org/ascended-masters/ All accessed August 2018

better than the Christian God, who I viewed as patriarchal, distant and unknowable. The New Age was so much better than the Christian religion, which to me was too narrow and non-accepting of all people. How many wars have been caused by religion? I used to think.

In reality, through my ignorance, I bought into a lie. I did not know Jesus personally as I do now. Because of this, I minimised the magnificence of the Creator of the Universe and His Son. When the true Jesus and the gospel are unknown, we are consequently not presented with the choice to accept Him as Lord and Saviour. The consequence of this is separation from God forever.

Who would want to be separated from our God of love, justice and judgment—in whom we can dwell safely and with absolute certainty that we are secure and loved? It was so important for me to trust that God is a good God to help heal the wound caused by the abusive behaviour of my husband. God is <u>totally trustworthy</u>—His character is flawless, and He <u>cannot lie</u>. There is no deception with God—deception is the hallmark of the enemy.

Keeping in mind that the enemy is a master of deceit and counterfeit, it then becomes clear how it can *appear* that the New Age philosophies are loving and harmless. The Bible provides a solid foundation for understanding what is of the light and what is of the darkness. For example, Scriptures such as *Acts 8:5-8*[70] (describing healing from God) and *Exodus 7:8-12*[71] (describing how magicians performed a 'miracle' but

---

[70] *Acts 8:5 Then Philip went down to the city of Samaria and preached Christ to them. 6 And the multitudes with one accord heeded the things spoken by Philip, hearing and seeing the miracles which he did. 7 For unclean spirits, crying with a loud voice, came out of many who were possessed; and many who were paralysed and lame were healed. 8 And there was great joy in that city.*

[71] *Exodus 7:8 Then the LORD spoke to Moses and Aaron, saying 9 "When Pharaoh speaks to you, saying, 'Show a miracle for yourselves,' then you shall say to Aaron, 'Take your rod and cast it before Pharaoh, and let it become a serpent. 10*

FROM NEW AGE TO NEW CREATION

God's miracle prevailed). Scripture provides extensive information about how the enemy deceives and how subtle this deception can be. Until I began to live Jesus' way, I had no idea as to the far-reaching nature of this deception.

God's plan for my life and for all those who believe in Him is a good one. The enemy's plan for my life and yours is *anything* but good. And we don't even have to believe in the enemy in order for his plan for our lives to be outworked. I did not know God. Nor did I have any idea of who I am in Christ and so I was, by default, following the enemy's plan. In order to follow God's good plan for our lives, we must accept Jesus into our hearts—for Jesus is the *only* way to the Heavenly Father. I'm talking about the **real Jesus**. Jesus—the One who *is* the way, the One who *is* the truth, the One who *is* the life. These are words you would expect to hear from One who is God. That He not only speaks the truth, Jesus IS truth. The New Age wanted me to be "true to myself" but Jesus wants me to be "true to truth". I'll say it again—Jesus IS truth.

To follow the enemy's plan, we must ignore Jesus. It's that simple. The mish-mash of beliefs and practices of the New Age teachings I followed were part of that *"wide gate and broad way that leads to destruction"*[72]. I was one of the many who entered—and who are still entering—through it. I was searching for relief and for answers to the questions I held in my mind. Unbeknown to me, and in my tryingness and brokenness, I was following the plan of the enemy.

So Moses and Aaron went in to Pharaoh, and they did so, just as the LORD commanded. And Aaron cast down his rod before Pharaoh and before his servants, and it became a serpent. 11 But Pharaoh also called the wise men and the sorcerers, so the magicians of Egypt, they also did in like manner with their enchantments. 12 For every man threw down his rod, and they became serpents. But Aaron's rod swallowed up their rods.

[72] *Matthew 7:13 Enter by the narrow gate. For wide is the gate and broad is the way that leads to destruction, and there are many who go in by it.*

It was the enemy who would fill my head with crippling, tormenting thoughts that reduced me to not only *identify* with my shame, but to be *defined* by my shame and guilt and the belief that I was less than and unlovable. These were thoughts of condemnation. Thoughts of condemnation <u>do not</u> come from God.

Am I rigid, dogmatic and intolerant because I believe in the one true God and follow Jesus? Tolerance is defined as "sympathy or indulgence for beliefs or practices differing from or conflicting with one's own"[73] and, to a certain extent, I believe this to be true. But it has limits. There is a moral code—created by God—that governs our view of what is right and wrong. This is what our society is built on. Morally, a paedophile's sexualising of a child is not "love" but is instead a sick and twisted perversion. To me, this is the most abhorrent and sinful behaviour. To God, this is sin. No single sin is greater or lesser than any other sin. Sin is sin. All sin is abhorrent to God.

Sin is the breaking of God's laws, as described in *1 John 3:4*[74]. And it is the sinful *behaviour* of each of us that Jesus came to address. I will repeat this—it is the sinful *behaviour* of each of us that Jesus came to address. Behaviour is *what we do*, not *who we are*. And who are we? We are His creations, created in His image and likeness, and as creations of God, we are loved more than we can imagine. When we accept Jesus, repenting of our sins and following Him, we are then <u>committed </u>to Him and His ways. And He is the *only* way to come to our Father God[75]. Jesus urges

---

[73] As defined in Merriam-Webster's Dictionary.

[74] *1 John 3:4 Whoever commits sin also commits lawlessness, and sin is lawlessness. 5 And you know that He was manifested to take away our sins, and in Him there is no sin.*

[75] *John 14:6 Jesus said to him, "I am the way, the truth, and the life. No one comes to the Father except through Me."*

us to love one another as He has first loved us. His love is made visible by the forgiveness of sin—the forgiveness of all that we have done or will do—that was His work at the Cross.

The choice as to how we behave is up to us. This is called free will and it is inbuilt into each created person. It is how God has designed us. Free will also means that we get to choose how we spend our lives—and how we spend Eternity. God would not force Himself on any of us and certainly, He would not force us to spend Eternity with Him if we do not want this. We choose either to be with our loving Lord God Almighty in Heaven or with Satan the deceiver in Hell.

In order for there to be true meaning, contrast and comparison must exist. There are "absolutes" in this world. Without darkness, there can be no light. Without a "no", a "yes" becomes meaningless. Without order, chaos ensues. I know life with Jesus and life without Him. Before I accepted Him into my heart, I thought I would have to be "perfect" in the sense that I would have to be straight-laced and morally self-righteous to be a "true Christian". I imagined being condemned by other Christians with their "holier-than-thou" attitudes if I tried to be like them. The truth was that I was the one with the "holier than thou" superior attitude. I thought I was better than those narrow-minded, boring Christians! I was too rebellious to ever be a Christian. I didn't want to conform or become like a sheep, blindly following the leader. Besides, I believed that there were many truths to be embraced in my journey of life. I also believed that through these many truths I would work out what *my* truth was.

I knew I fell short. I knew that I was far from perfect. But New Age teachings deceived me into thinking that I could *become* perfect (as in being self-realised). I wanted to be accepted for who I was, but I did not see how acceptance of someone like me and Christianity could possibly be compatible with each other.

These were my patterns of thought. Nothing could be further from the truth.

I didn't realise the narrow way to Jesus—asking Him to come into my heart—was the only way to finding real, perfect love and acceptance. All of my thinking about what it meant to believe in God was faulty. God was not this vast, impersonal, unapproachable deity sitting way up there in Heaven. Through Jesus, God became personal to me.

I hadn't had much to do with other Christians who had accepted Jesus as their Lord and Saviour and become "born again". I only remembered the Christianity of my childhood, which was a religion rather than a relationship. I didn't realise that being a Christian was surrendering to the One who created me and who loved me in all of my brokenness and humanness. I didn't realise that being a Christian meant making a commitment to follow Jesus.

What I also did not also realise was that it was not just about me—and in truth, it never had been. Rather, it was all about living in a world that could deny God's love for his children. A world where the perfect bond between our Heavenly Father and His children had been severed. It was all about our Father God providing a way forward for the restoration of this bond and His loving relationship with His children. Through Jesus. Through the sacrifice of Jesus on the Cross. Through redemptive Jesus and what He did for all of mankind.

This Jesus was a man—a real person. History records that Jesus existed as a man and that He died on a Cross. The gospel of Luke, one of the books in the New Testament, speaks about Jesus and the movement of Christianity in a historical context. History also records that He rose from the dead after three days and that he was sighted by, and interacted with, many people[76]. But history cannot provide proof (that Jesus is who He says He is) to someone who is not ready to accept Jesus into their hearts and lives. Had I waited until I had proof that Jesus could transform me and my life—the way he had done for my friend who led me to Him—I would still be unsaved. It was a step of faith that I could either take—or not take. I would still have belonged, unknowingly and by default, to the enemy. I would still have been living, unwittingly, in the Kingdom of Darkness—instead of being cradled in the arms of the Light of the World.

---

[76] *The Case for Christ - A Journalist's Personal Investigation of the Evidence for Jesus"* – by Lee Strobel, Zondervan 1998 p. 316 – Jesus' appearances after the Resurrection.

CHAPTER 8

The Original and the Best

Proverbs 30:5 *Every word of God is pure; He is a shield to those who put their trust in Him.*

Proverbs 23:7 *"For as he thinks in his heart, so is he".*

Matthew 7:7 *"Ask, and it will be given to you; seek, and you will find; knock, and it will be opened to you".*

Philippians 4:8 *Finally, brethren, whatever things are true, whatever things are noble, whatever things are just, whatever things are pure, whatever things are lovely, whatever things are of good report, if there is any virtue and if there is anything praiseworthy—meditate on these things.*

One of the most prominent of New Age teachings is the power of positive thinking. This is a doctrine invented by Norman Vincent Peale[77] which taught that obstacles and difficulties in life can be overcome by the power of the mind and by "thinking positive". Many of the most popular and well-known statements of positive thinking are in fact plagiarised Scriptures from the Bible (for example, those cited at the start of this chapter). Scriptures are the original and the "positive thinking" counterpart are the counterfeits. When I was into New Age, I

---

[77] https://en.wikipedia.org/wiki/Norman_Vincent_Peale

was someone who "thought positive" and had a "positive mindset"—exalting myself as the author and master of my own destiny.

The Holy Bible, however, firmly sets God—our Creator and the One who holds all the pieces of the puzzle that is His good plan for our lives—in the position of authority (*John 15:5 I am the vine, you are the branches. He who abides in Me, and I in him, bears much fruit; for without Me you can do nothing*). The Holy Bible is the ultimate handbook, providing guidance for every single situation in life. But unless there is faith in God and consequently the illumination of His Holy Spirit, the Bible will not be revealed as it truly is—the masterpiece of God's breathed and living ordained word.

Scripture honours and glorifies our Creator as our authority and the source from which all is created. As well as the mind, God looks at the heart, through Jesus's sacrifice on the Cross. His work in us is to transform and heal the heart. Jesus came to restore the relationship between man and God once and for all so that there is no more separation. The things of the mind *and* the heart are renewed in Christ Jesus.

Renewal of the mind goes far beyond "thinking positive". And in order for the positive to exist, there must also be negative. Dark and light. Good and evil. Right and wrong. That is the truth. As followers of Jesus, we are to meditate on those things which are praiseworthy and beautiful, as instructed in Philippians 4:8. We are also to acknowledge and recognise that there will be trouble in the world but also recognise the victory in the One who has overcome—*John 16:33 "These things I have spoken to you, that in Me you may have peace. In the world you will have tribulation; but be of good cheer, I have overcome the world."*

In Jesus, we have the promise and the authority that He has overcome the world. So, to put our trust in Him means that we have peace in, and are able to trust, the One who will take on our challenges and help us—

no matter what circumstances in our lives we are presented with. After Jesus had overcome death and appeared to the apostles, the Holy Spirit was made available for guidance[78]. It is the Holy Spirit which opens our minds, helping us to understand the Bible and how to live God's way. Living God's way means becoming familiar with His character, His instructions for life and His promises for us.

God's heart is for His children and His love for us is unfailing. For example, we know through Scripture that His plan for our lives is good[79] and, as our Creator, He knows everything there is to know about us[80]. He is also able to do much, much more than we can ask for or think, according to the power of His Holy Spirit, that works within us[81]. And, as followers of Jesus and modelling His teachings we are able to make a huge impact on our world through His ministry of reconciliation with God[82].

There are many, many other Scriptures that speak of God's love for us and His promises of goodness for our lives. Think about this—God has created and fashioned each one of us uniquely, with a specific and good

---

[78] *Luke 24:45 And He opened their understanding, that they might comprehend the Scriptures.*

[79] *Jeremiah 29:11 "For I know the thoughts that I think toward you, says the LORD, thoughts of peace and not of evil, to give you a future and a hope. 12 Then you will call upon Me and go and pray to Me, and I will listen to you. 13 And you will seek Me and find Me, when you search for Me with all your heart.*

[80] *Psalm 139:13 For You formed my inward parts; You covered me in my mother's womb. 14 I will praise You, for I am fearfully and wonderfully made; Marvellous are Your works, And that my soul knows very well.*

[81] *Ephesians 3:20 Now to Him who is able to do exceedingly abundantly above all that we ask or think, according to the power that works in us.*

[82] *2 Corinthians 5:18 Now all things are of God, who has reconciled us to Himself through Jesus Christ, and has given us the ministry of reconciliation.*

plan for each of our lives. He has written a blueprint for our lives through His Holy Bible and has provided a way—through our acceptance of Jesus—that we can never again be separated from Him.

Think about this—the Creator of this world and the entire universe, Who is all powerful and all knowing, loving, just and merciful, wants so much to be in relationship with each of His creations (friend, that's you and me). But only if this is *freely* chosen and reciprocated.

Our Father God wants us to come to Him *freely* to achieve every part of His good plan for our lives. He has uniquely and especially created us for this purpose and for His glory. In order for His plan for us to be achieved, it is required that we choose *freely* to walk with Him to become our authentic selves. As we walk with Him in obedience, we naturally discover our gifts and talents. Not being who God created us to be will simply not do!

Can you imagine being who you are truly created to be, living the way of an all-powerful God who loves you so much that He sent His only Son to die for you? I find this to be both an excitingly nerve-wracking prospect as well as a massive challenge and honour to serve the One who created me. At the end of my life, I so want to hear Him say those words in *Matthew 25:35 "Well done, good and faithful servant"*.

The gift of grace[83] and relationship with Jesus is free. However, this is not to say that there is no price that must be paid. Becoming a child of God and resolving and determining to live His way is no easy feat in this day and age, in a culture that is counter to so many of His teachings. However, to be in His presence and journey with Him, to have my identity in Him rather than in what the world says I should be is a price that I willingly choose to pay.

---

[83] https://www.biblestudytools.com/dictionary/grace/ Accessed August 2018

FROM NEW AGE TO NEW CREATION

I have reached a point, through being on this journey with Jesus, that I can now be grateful for what I learned from my abusive marriage. Had it not been so painful and dark, I may not have found the light that is Jesus. I know I was searching for answers as to why I had come to be in such a dark place. I could no longer simply "think positive". I was too exhausted and trapped to visualise and create a new and positive reality for myself.

Because I had lost hope, I did not have the strength nor the energy to be *able* to even know where to start to create a new reality. Instead, what I needed was to *find* a reality that was outside of myself and my circumstances—that did not require any strength of mind on my behalf. I did not realise it at the time but what I needed was to go beyond what my mind was telling me, into the realm of allowing my heart to open up to a new perspective. And this was very scary for me, as my heart was so fragile and hurting.

It wasn't just a matter of leaving the abusive marriage—I had done that before, half a dozen times, and been drawn back in, like a spider's prey being drawn into its web. I truly felt so hopeless and trapped, as though a poison had seeped into my system that was systematically paralysing me. Each time I was drawn back in, I lost a little more of my self until it became impossible for me to believe that I could permanently break free of my abusive situation.

Each time I left and returned, my mind was being programmed a little more to be a victim. I struggled to survive and be present for my children.

Being a victim in an abusive marriage meant I no longer believed I had *any* ability to change my own life. It meant I no longer believed I was entitled to peace or dignity. Being in the grip and control of my ex-husband meant, at a very deep level, that I no longer believed I had worth or meaning to my life. I existed simply to go through the motions of being in that marriage, where everything was set up for the comfort of one person alone. I mothered my children as best I could, but we were all shell-shocked victims of an abuser who was tormented endlessly within his own mind and who, in turn, tormented those closest to him. We all lived in the grip of the enemy.

When I asked Jesus into my heart (and was received into *His* heart), He took that effort and that burden away. I found hope again through Him, through who He is and what He did for me on the Cross. He gave me that hope again. His forgiveness set me free. His promises and the love that I experienced through being in relationship with Him slowly began to rebuild what was shattered within me. Because He is the Creator and therefore powerful and limitless, He reached into the very depths of my being and shone His supernatural light into the shadows that had all but engulfed me.

I now had a lifeline 24/7 where all I had to do was ask and I would receive the guidance and love and healing I had so desperately craved. This time, it was 100% genuine, authentic and tailored especially for me.

CHAPTER 9

Jesus – The Way, the Truth, and the Life

__Psalm 107:9__ For He satisfies the longing soul. And fills the hungry soul with goodness.

__1 Timothy 4:1__ Now the Spirit expressly says that in latter times some will depart from the faith, giving heed to deceiving spirits and doctrines of demons.

__2 Thessalonians 2:9__ The coming of the lawless one will be in accordance with how Satan works. He will use all sorts of displays of power through signs and wonders that serve the lie, 10 and all the ways that wickedness deceives those who are perishing. They perish because they refused to love the truth and so be saved. 11 For this reason God sends them a powerful delusion so that they will believe the lie 12 and so that all will be condemned who have not believed the truth but have delighted in wickedness.

I have often been guilty of reading a book and then part of the way through suddenly skipping to the ending. I don't want to wait to know how things turn out. The same is true for my life—I don't want to wait to know how things turn out! I wonder how my life will end up and whether I will have made a difference to my world.

As one who loves to skip to the ending of a book, I am satisfied that I now know the ending to my story—my own Book of Life. I know this through Scripture and I believe this through my relationship with, and commitment to, Jesus. I know that I will be in Heaven, spending Eternity with Jesus. I think of His face—His wonderful face! I imagine what this will be like. The Bible tells me that I now live in Him and so my life is to be a testimony and testament to His goodness and grace.

The Bible tells me I live within a Creator who created me and all the days of my life before there was even one of them. This is written in *Psalm 139:15 My frame was not hidden from You, When I was made in secret, And skilfully wrought in the lowest parts of the earth. 16 Your eyes saw my substance, being yet unformed, And in Your book they all were written, The days fashioned for me, When as yet there were none of them"*. We are not mistakes and we are not accidents—we are intentionally created, with our own unique story written before we are even born.

To me, this is the most soothing balm to the woundedness of my soul.

Scripture reassures me that, as a child of God, there is no more aloneness or isolation. One such Scripture of many is the beautiful *Psalm 147:3 He heals the brokenhearted And binds up their wounds. 4 He counts the number of the stars; He calls them all by name. 5 Great is our Lord, and mighty in power; His understanding is infinite.*

It has been a major part of my journey to begin to realise that I am not alone. When I wrote my first book—*Hearing His Voice—Meeting Jesus in the Garden of Promise: A Devotional Journey of Encouragement*[84]—I was going through a very hard and challenging time and feeling very alone. During the process of writing the book, Jesus gave me a revelation that He was with me and for me. This was a huge blessing, which emerged from a time of great distress. That's God! Doing things for our ultimate good and His glory.

---

[84] http://www.amazon.com/dp/B075HHRNPG

FROM NEW AGE TO NEW CREATION

As a child of God, with a *revelation* of being His child, I know there is no isolation nor separation from Him[85]. I choose to trust Jesus and to seek Him, to stay close to Him—in fact, to cling to Him. In this way, even when it appears as though He is not with me, He is always available. He is always available through His written word (the Bible) and the revelatory guide of His Holy Spirit. He is always available through prayer.

Jesus is also a clear focus. We are told in Scripture that all things are created through Him and by Him. There are not multiple teachers, multiple books nor multiple works needed to remake that which is entrusted to Him and which He knows intimately—us. Therefore, the path we follow with Him is very clear—simple yet profound. There is no trial and error. It is a tried and true formula that has stood the test of time: pray, worship, praise, obey, read Scripture, listen for the Holy Spirit, meditate on His word. Coming from the place of a sincere heart. Rinse and repeat.

My identity in Jesus means I have a firm foundation for my life, a centeredness that sees me take up my Cross and carry it. This is known as dying to self. New Age celebrates the self as being the ultimate authority. Jesus celebrates the self too, but as being unique, fearfully and wonderfully created by Him and who He knows intimately, right down to knowing every hair on our heads.

However, Jesus does not elevate the knowledge and love of the self above all else. He is the way, the truth and the life, encouraging selflessness and love for one another. He asks us to love one another as He has loved us. When our identity is firmly rooted in Christ, the need for approval from others gradually loses its appeal.

---

[85] *Deuteronomy 31:6 Be strong and of good courage, do not fear nor be afraid of them; for the LORD your God, He is the One who goes with you. He will not leave you nor forsake you.*

My relationship with Jesus is not only for comfort or something to make me feel better. Feelings come and go. I do, however, always feel comforted and better through spending time with Him. My relationship with Him is not only because I believe in Him and have faith He is real. My relationship with Jesus goes deeper than comfort, faith and belief in that it is one of **personal revelation**. I am personally committed to Him. He is the foundation of my life because I have personally experienced His love for me. I have personally experienced his transforming power in my life. I continue to do so.

For example, right now I am struggling with being consistent. I have worries about money because my income is sporadic at the moment. My weight goes up and down as I eat for comfort. I realise that I am basing my sense of security and wellbeing on external things like having enough money and looking my best. What I am learning now is to instead base my sense of security on Jesus. By reinforcing my knowledge of His promises and through the journey of relationship with Him, I give Jesus the opportunity to demonstrate His faithfulness and provision in every area of my life.

For me, this is definitely an ongoing lesson and I resist learning it regularly. I regularly go back to my old ways. However, Jesus is faithful, and He allows me to recommit time and time again. His grace is precious, and it is His forgiveness and infinite patience with me that sees the transformation of what are, for me, some very real strongholds in my life.

In a world where there are many distractions and many different things to see, do and explore, and much restlessness, Jesus is the rock that is never changing and always faithful. Having a relationship with Him has given me great emotional stability. And I am getting better at being thankful for the learning available in all circumstances—good and bad[86]!

Other religions and New Age give good advice about what to do. Christianity and the Bible give good advice about what to do (especially the Book of Proverbs) but also good news about what has been *done* already—that is, what Jesus did at the Cross. That Jesus, God's only Son, came to Earth as a man and died on a Cross as He took on all of humankind's sins. Jesus became the ultimate sacrifice—He *became* sin—so that we may be forgiven of our sins and restore our relationship with God. After three days, Jesus rose again. Death was overcome. The gift of salvation (no more separation from God but living with Him in Heaven forever) was freely given to us when we accepted the One who loves us so perfectly—and Who, sometime in the future, will return to Earth again.

The gift of salvation and a relationship with Jesus are, in fact, so life-changing that countless Christians have been, and still are, willing to suffer intense persecution for their faith. For instance, all of the apostles except John died very gruesome deaths[87]. In more modern times, two men who suffered unimaginable persecutions are Richard Wurmbrand[88], founder of The Voice of the Martyrs, and Brother Yun[89], one of the foremost leaders (now exiled) of China's house churches. There are many, many others.

---

[86] *1 Thessalonians 5:18 in everything give thanks; for this is the will of God in Christ Jesus for you.*

[87] http://channel.nationalgeographic.com/killing-jesus/articles/how-did-the-apostles-die/

[88] https://relevantmagazine.com/culture/richard-wurmbrand-tortured-christ-remained-faithful/ Both accessed August 2018.

[89] http://www.inspirationalchristians.org/biography/brother-yun/ Accessed August 2018

I ask myself: why would this be? Why would anyone want to suffer, even to the point of death, for their faith (but without murdering others in the process?). Why would anyone want to follow a carpenter whose ministry only lasted three years? The answer, of course, is that the carpenter is who He says He is—God's only begotten Son, the Saviour of the world, whose miracles were so many that they could not all be included in the Bible[90].

For the most part, I do not want to imagine my life without Jesus. Yet there have been times in the past, and no doubt there will times in the future, when I have questioned my faith, especially when life is hard. I have had times where my faith felt meaningless because of the lies of the enemy filling my mind. I would be crying out to Jesus yet unsure as to whether He was really present. These times were temporary and soon passed as I leaned closer to Jesus and allowed Him to work with me. As *Hebrews 11:1* says: *Now faith is the substance of things hoped for, the evidence of things not seen.*

This questioning is part of the transformational process and there are stages of faith on the Christian journey[91]. God, our God of love, justice and judgement, is well equipped to handle any questions we may have. The image that comes to my mind when I think of not having Jesus in my life is like a lonely wind howling across a desolate landscape. I repent for these thoughts, but I am secure in His love that He is okay with this. Because He is God and I am not! He has given me *everything*. He

---

[90] *John 21:25 And there are also many other things that Jesus did, which if they were written one by one, I suppose that even the world itself could not contain the books that would be written. Amen.*

[91] The Critical Journey – Stages in the Life of Faith by Janet O. Hagberg and Robert A. Guelich, 2nd Edition, Sheffield Publishing Company, Salem Wisconsin, 1995

continues to give me everything and because of this, with each passing day, I want to serve Him and glorify Him with how I live my life.

I used to pride myself on not being "one of the sheep" and to now find myself obedient to the One who is the supreme Shepherd—Jesus—is something I never would have believed possible. He does not require anything except our free will choice to accept Him. The desire to be obedient and to follow His ways are a natural consequence of experiencing His deep love. I could never have imagined being obedient would be so transforming and so freeing. It's not an obedience of just "toeing the line"—although we are given clear guidance in the Bible on how to live—rather, it is an obedience of wanting to do my best for My Saviour.

This is because he has radically transformed me! This is because He has tenderly taken my frozen little heart and warmed it up in His mighty hands. And this is because the magnitude of what it took for Him to save one such as me is something I will never be able to comprehend. As a natural outflow of this, I *want* to be obedient to Him and seek His ways. I want to know Him. I know He loves me—although I am unlikely to realise the depth of His love.

God is a God of love and also of justice. Because of this, discipline and accountability are essential in my walk and all the instructions are, again, found in Scripture. Being authentic and vulnerable in order to yield to Jesus is also essential on the walk with Him. Therefore, being with other believers, being honest about our pain and shortcomings and taking the necessary steps in accordance with His way, is very important. Praying for each other and the ministering of the Holy Spirit are powerful tools in our walk. Disciplines such as fasting to be closer to Him are also very important. I find this a hard challenge as one of my struggles is with food and emotional eating but again, as I walk with Jesus and keep recommitting my struggles in this area to Him, I have faith that this will be overcome. I am still alive, so I know my race is not yet finished! (*Philippians 3:14 I press toward the goal for the prize of the upward call of God in Christ Jesus*).

I realise that, in writing these words, I am doing my best to express the profound transformation I experience through my relationship with Jesus. I am doing my best to express the depth and magnitude of what I have found in my relationship with Jesus. I fall short. There really are no words to adequately express this.

I am only one person whose life has been totally transformed by meeting Jesus. There are many accounts of others, both in the Bible and throughout history. One such radical transformation, described in the Bible, is the story of the Apostle Paul. Paul used to be known as Saul (meaning to ask, inquire, borrow or beg) of Tarsus. We first meet him in the Bible in *Acts Chapter 7:58* where he was guarding the clothes of the people responsible for stoning Stephen the martyr.

His persecution of Christians is documented in *Acts 8:3 "As for Saul, he made havoc of the church, entering every house, and dragging off men and women, committing them to prison."* We meet him again in *Chapter 9:1 "Then Saul, still breathing threats and murder against the disciples of the Lord, went to the high priest, 2 and asked letters from him to the synagogues of Damascus, so that if he found any who were of the Way, whether men or women, he might bring them bound to Jerusalem."* Acts 9:3-31 continues on with the story of Saul the persecutor of Jesus (*Acts 9:3 As he journeyed he came near Damascus, and suddenly a light shone around him from heaven. 4 Then he fell to the ground, and heard a voice saying to him, "Saul, Saul, why are you persecuting Me?"*).

Saul's transformation into Paul (meaning humble or small) the radical evangelist of Jesus is a truly amazing story of one who was totally against Christianity, having a personal encounter with Lord Jesus and being completely and radically converted. His letters to the churches make up much of the New Testament—Galatians, 1 and 2 Thessalonians, 1 and 2

FROM NEW AGE TO NEW CREATION

Corinthians, Romans, Ephesians, Philemon, Colossians and Philippians, and 2 Timothy and Titus, between AD 47 and 64[92].

There are thousands, if not millions, of accounts of people like Saul having a supernatural, personal encounter with the risen One.

I personally know of many such people and there are countless others on websites www.WashedRed.com/changed_lives/ or www.IamSecond.com. There are many well-known evangelists such as Greg Laurie[93] and Joyce Meyer[94] who each have amazing testimonies of how their lives have been transformed by accepting Jesus into their hearts. Type "People who have been transformed by an encounter with Jesus" into your search engine and see the wealth of information which comes up.

At the core of this transformation is the love of Jesus—the real and pure love of the Creator for His created masterpiece. Each of us is His created masterpiece. Each of us is given the opportunity to accept Him, to allow for His love to come into the deepest part of us, the most shrivelled and terrified part that aches with a formless and nameless pain that cannot be defined. This pain is ancient and profound and it began at the dawn of time through evil entering a garden of beauty and infecting a good creation.

The idea of reincarnation and the soul evolving does not include Heaven spent with a Creator. It does not include the one life of worth

---

[92] www.gotquestions.org/how-many-books-did-Paul-write.html

[93] https://www.oneplace.com/ministries/a-new-beginning/listen/the-power-of-a-personal-testimony-2-38754.html

https://www.oneplace.com/ministries/a-new-beginning/listen/the-power-of-a-personal-testimony-3-38755.html All accessed August 2018

[94] http://blog.godreports.com/2017/06/joyce-meyer-overcame-abuse-by-her-father-led-him-to-christ-years-later Accessed August 2018

and validity designed for the glory and honour of its Creator. Each person is made in the image of God and each person has the opportunity to come back to God. Free will means God will not force this on anyone. The gift of grace through the death and resurrection of Jesus at the Cross is one freely given to those who choose to accept Him as their Lord and Saviour. God's love is great, permanent, lasting and eternal. His plan is for none to be separated from Him.

I came to a point in my life where I had to be honest with myself and ask myself what I truly wanted. Do I keep living life the way I have been, or do I take a chance on committing myself to living life differently, with a completely different foundation? *Can* I live life differently? Do I believe for an eternal life in Heaven with our Creator? Do I think I can have enough faith to follow Jesus? Am I willing to sacrifice how I live my life to experience the love of a Saviour who was willing to die for me? And who is now alive for me?

My sacrifice was my need to control. It was my fear. It was my belief that I was a good person with an eternal soul and did not need Jesus. It was my pride that I had all the answers. And if I didn't have them, I would surely be able to find them.

God's sacrifice was his only Son. Jesus' sacrifice was His life. Everything He had. He gave it willingly. He is the answer to every question that cries out from the deep and aching void of a terrified and lonely heart.

And when the Saviour entered my heart, He took away that terror and loneliness. He soothed my heart and ministered to it. He grew me in ways that were at times so uncomfortable but so necessary for me. And over time, I surrendered my trust to Him. I learned and experienced firsthand His trustworthiness and faithfulness, and because of this, my trust in Him grew exponentially.

FROM NEW AGE TO NEW CREATION

So I don't *have* to do for Him, but I *want* to do for Him. My faith in Him as the King of Kings means that I declare that He is greater than any obstacle I might face in this life. I don't ignore or deny the obstacle. I declare Jesus is greater and can meet all my needs. I believe in His promises and give Him the glory and honour for whatever I have and achieve in this life, as well as that which is to come. (*Romans 4:17 . . . in the presence of Him who he believed—God, who gives life to the dead and calls those things which do not exist as though they did*") I do my best to follow the teaching of *Mark 12:30 Love the Lord your God with all your heart and with all your soul and with all your strength.*

To accept Jesus is to find the way, the truth, and the life[95]. Christianity was originally known as the Way[96]. We have a Saviour who has given us an instructional guidebook for our life and directions on how to live it. We are to *"Love the LORD your God with all your heart, with all your soul, with all your strength, and with all your mind*; and to *'love your neighbour as yourself'"* (*Luke 10:27*).

This is completely counter-cultural to the "me first" society we live in. Even though the idea of servant leadership is gaining credence, unless the foundation of this is the original servant leader, Jesus[97], the *foundation* is not solid and the end result *without* God is eternal separation *from* God.

As has been discussed in previous chapters, New Age has counterfeited many practices which were originally described in the Bible. One such practice is meditation. The practice of meditation in The Bible is

---

[95] *John 14:6 Jesus answered, "I am the way and the truth and the life. No one comes to the Father except through Me."*

[96] References to early followers of Christ being known as followers of the Way are described in *Acts 9:2; 19:9, 23; 22:4; 24:14* and *22*.

[97] *Matthew 20:28 "just as the Son of Man did not come to be served, but to serve, and to give His life a ransom for many.*

mentioned extensively[98]. It is clear that meditation is to be on God and His Holy Word. When I practised meditation in the New Age (for example, during the Buddhist Vipassana retreat, as part of Siddha Yoga or imagining a spirit guide coming to me), I was emptying my mind in some way. And an empty mind presents a doorway ripe for the enemy to enter. Unknowingly, I was inviting ungodly things into the realm of my mind. In contrast, in Scripture, we are taught how to *renew our mind*[99]. We are given the *mind of Christ*[100].

In my experience, hand in hand with meditation was yoga, which for many years I avidly practised. It very much helped my back injury and got my body flexible. When I first accepted Jesus I was still happy to practise yoga—to me, it was "just stretching". I saw it as a healthful practice which focused on stretching and balancing the body in harmony with the breath.

It may appear to be "just stretching"—purely physical—but there is a spiritual core to Yoga which invites different gods into us through the poses. For example, Salute to the Sun is a series of different poses which essentially worship the sun god. Taken in this context, yoga is essentially a practice to open your mind and body to the spirit realm. And herein lies the danger for Christians embracing yoga as a form of exercise.

---

[98] Meditation on Scriptures (by no means an exhaustive list): *Psalm 1:1-3; Psalm 19:4; Psalm 104:1-34; Philippians 4:8; 2 Timothy 2:7, Psalm 16:8; Psalm 63:6; Psalm 119:15-16; Joshua 1:8; Psalm 77:12; Psalm 111:2; Psalm 143:5; Psalm 145:5; Psalm 8:1-9; Proverbs 6:6; Matthew 6:26-30; Luke 12:24-27; Psalm 119:11; 55; and 78-148; Psalm 16:7; Psalm 42:8; Job 22:22; Psalm 39:3; Luke 2:19; Acts 8:27-35.*

[99] *Romans 12:2 And do not be conformed to this world, but be transformed by the renewing of your mind, that you may prove what is that good and acceptable and perfect will of God.*

[100] *1 Corinthians 2:16 For "who has known the mind of the Lord that he may instruct Him?" But we have the mind of Christ.*

FROM NEW AGE TO NEW CREATION

There is inherent potential for harm—for putting other gods before our God. As we are instructed in *Exodus 20:3 You shall have no other gods before me*.

The origins of yoga are very ancient. The Sanskrit word 'yuj', literally meaning to yoke or to bind, is the root word for yoga. The English root word is also 'yuj'[101]. The word yoga comes from the word "yoke". In *Matthew 11:29-30*[102] Jesus asks us to take His yoke upon us and learn from Him. In biblical times, yoking occurred when two oxen were bound together to draw the plough. So, Jesus invites us to walk with Him as in being yoked together.

As a Christian, I want to open up to the yoke of Jesus, which provides comfort and rest—and not to the yoke of yoga, which invokes unseen spirits. There is no middle ground—it is either one or the other. I can't have both. Once again, I go back to looking at the root of something—and questioning whether this root is godly or not. We are instructed in Scripture that the body is to be presented as a living sacrifice, holy and pleasing to God. We are to care for our bodies, nourish them and exercise them, but not in a way that is dishonourable to our Creator God[103].

God as the Creator of all creation is worshiped and revered with every aspect of our lives. His creation includes the Universe. True, it is a vast

---

[101] *"Dealing with Python: The Spirit of Constriction: Strategies for the Threshold #1"*, by Anne Hamilton, Armour Books (2017).

[102] *Matthew 11:29 "Take My yoke upon you and learn from Me, for I am gentle and lowly in heart, and you will find rest for your souls. 30 For My yoke is easy and My burden is light."*

[103] *Romans 12:1 I beseech you therefore, brethren, by the mercies of God, that you present your bodies a living sacrifice, holy, acceptable to God, which is your reasonable service.*

and immense creation beyond the scope of our limited human minds[104] but it is still something that is **created**. It is not the **Creator**[105]. When I think about this now, I wonder why I ever believed that the Universe was the place where things could come to fruition. How could I focus on something so vast? Why would I ask a collection of stars and galaxies for what I wanted?

I used to see myself as a "co-creator" with the Universe, an equal partner, so to speak, to bring everything I desired into worldly reality. I did not think about the One who was Creator of myself, the Universe and everything and everyone else in existence. I simply did not think that I could be created intentionally, by a loving Creator. My view was that I was a human child created by and born of human parents—not a child of God created by Him and born of human parents. It did not enter my head to believe that I was a created masterpiece spoken so lovingly of in the Scriptures.

The majesty of God Himself is vast and all-encompassing. He is the Creator responsible for all creation, including the Universe and all Universal laws (e.g. the law of gravity). We can know of His character through Scripture and through our relationship with Him and His Son Jesus but it is an impossibility to define One who is so majestically undefinable.

---

[104] https://www.collinsdictionary.com/dictionary/english/universe

[105] *Romans 1:25 who exchanged the truth of God for the lie, and worshiped and served the creature rather than the Creator, who is blessed forever. Amen.*

CONCLUSION

God pursues us! One of the most powerful Psalms in the Bible is *Psalm 139*, written by David, where we read that, before we ever pursued God, He was pursuing us. I personally find this to be so incredibly inspiring and powerful. The Creator of the Universe pursuing me—and you—because He wants to be in relationship with us. He Who knows absolutely everything about us, and who, despite all of our frailties and inconsistencies, loves us so profoundly.

I find *Psalm 139*, written by King David, to be a powerful encapsulation of God's perfect knowledge of man. I have quoted parts of this Psalm earlier in this story. Here it is now, in all its glorious entirety.

Psalm 139

1 *You have searched me, LORD,*

    and you know me.

2 *You know when I sit and when I rise;*

    You perceive my thoughts from afar.

3 *You discern my going out and my lying down;*

    You are familiar with all my ways.

4 *Before a word is on my tongue*

    You, LORD, know it completely.

5 You hem me in behind and before,

    and You lay Your hand upon me.

6 Such lofty knowledge is too wonderful for me,

    Too lofty for me to attain.

7 Where can I go from your Spirit?

    Where can I flee from your presence?

8 If I go up to the heavens, you are there;

    If I make my bed in the depths, you are there.

9 If I rise on the wings of the dawn,

    If I settle on the far side of the sea,

10 even there your hand will guide me,

    Your right hand will hold me fast.

11 If I say, "Surely the darkness will hide me

    and the light become night around me,"

12 even the darkness will not be dark to you;

    the night will shine like the day,

    for darkness is as light to you.

13 For you created my inmost being;

    You knit me together in my mother's womb.

14 I praise you because I am fearfully and wonderfully made;

    Your works are wonderful,

    I know that full well.

15 My frame was not hidden from you

FROM NEW AGE TO NEW CREATION

> *when I was made in the secret place,*
>
> *when I was woven together in the depths of the earth.*

16 *Your eyes saw my unformed body;*

> *all the days ordained for me were written in your book*
>
> *before one of them came to be.*

17 *How precious to me are your thoughts, God!*

> *How vast is the sum of them!*

18 *Were I to count them,*

> *they would outnumber the grains of sand—*
>
> *when I awake, I am still with you.*

19 *If only you, God, would slay the wicked!*

> *Away from me, you who are bloodthirsty!*

20 *They speak of you with evil intent;*

> *Your adversaries misuse your name.*

21 *Do I not hate those who hate you, LORD,*

> *and abhor those who are in rebellion against you?*

22 *I have nothing but hatred for them;*

> *I count them my enemies.*

23 *Search me, God, and know my heart;*

> *test me and know my anxious thoughts.*

24 *See if there is any offensive way in me,*

> *and lead me in the way everlasting.*

Our God seeks us and finds us, using people, places and things to draw us to Him. He has made everything and everyone. There is nothing that is outside the scope of His power. And there is nothing our Heavenly Father wants more than to be in relationship with His children.

My hope is that you have seen, through my story, how God has transformed my life—radically! How He is still transforming my life with His gentle, faithful ways. I am so much a work in progress! I do not know *what* my future holds but I do know *Who* my future holds—and Who holds my future. I am learning who I am because I trust Whose I am. This is an ongoing process and one I do not expect will finish until I come face to face with Jesus and Father God in Heaven.

New Age teachings and philosophy without a doubt sustained me and helped me grow in many ways. I will always be grateful for this time in my life. I met many amazing people and felt a sense of fulfilment I had never felt before. Yet I see now that this sense of fulfilment was built on foundations of deception. I was deceived, accepting the principles of New Age at face value, when its roots were not godly. The love and light I thought were real was an illusion and the God-shaped hole, created in me when I was created, was not filled by it. And, unbeknownst to me, my eternal soul was at stake!

I found accepting Jesus was a step I was ready to take but I still needed to find the courage to take it. You have read where I said I felt very fearful. I was turning my back on all that I had known and journeying into uncharted territory. I wondered what changes in my life might happen once I was saved and born again? Would I turn strange? Would it be boring? Was it a trap? How could I possibly be obedient to Jesus? That felt a bit weird. What would it be like to read the Bible? I had tried and failed before to consistently read the Bible. Could I possibly—after all that I had done and been through—be acceptable to God? Would He—could He—love me? What did it mean to praise and worship God?

FROM NEW AGE TO NEW CREATION

What exactly did it mean to follow Jesus? Why did I feel so uncomfortable when I heard the word "sin"? I had so many questions without answers! And that gripping feeling of fear could easily have stopped me from accepting Jesus.

I accepted Jesus despite the uncertainty and despite the fear. What I stepped into was no trap, but a relationship of such love and personal growth, tailor-made for me with the loving Saviour available 24/7. I am still being developed and grown in ways I could never have imagined—all stemming from being saved by the amazing grace of Jesus[106]. He has set me free from the chains of my past which once had bound and shackled me.

There is nothing I have done or can do in the future that is the reason I am so loved by Jesus. I am loved by Him because of who He is and for what He has done on the Cross. Think of how people react when they see a baby. The baby doesn't have to do anything very special nor be anything other than who they are to have people goo-ing and gah-ing over its presence. People look at the baby and instantly there is a reaction. I think—and Scripture and my own experience with Him back this up—that is how God thinks of me and you.

I don't have to do anything special. I don't have to be anyone other than who I am. Who I am is enough. And that is who He wants me to be. Who I am. The me who He created. I am unique. Just as you are.

Jesus anchors me and lifts me up at the same time. Being in relationship with Jesus is like breathing a big sigh of relief. It's like taking a sweet, full

---

[106] *Ephesians 2:8-9 For by grace you have been saved through faith, and that not of yourselves; it is the gift of God, 9 not of works, lest anyone should boast. 10 For we are His workmanship, created in Christ Jesus for good works, which God prepared beforehand that we should walk in them.*

breath in and a slow, surrendering exhalation out. I can relax. I can trust Him.

Naturally, in sharing my story of how I came to faith, it is my fervent hope and prayer that you—if you don't already know Jesus—will want to experience the transformation that relationship with Him brings. This is not because I want people to be like me. It is because I want people to be like Him. Because He transforms completely—from the inside out.

And here's what I know and can promise you—His transforming power is here for you too. And He is waiting for you to acknowledge Him. To put your faith in Him and to allow Him to move into your heart. So that you can then come into His heart. He is waiting with His arms open and outstretched—for you to run into them. Waiting . . . to bring you Home.

His peace be with you.

Asking Jesus into Your Heart

If you don't yet have a relationship with Jesus Christ, but would like to do so, you can repeat the following simple prayer:

"Lord Jesus, I want to know you. I want you to come into my life and put things right. I know I have not lived my life with you in charge and I want to do that now. I am sorry that I have sinned. I repent of this and seek to live in a new way with You. Please come into my life and into my heart now and let me be with you always. Thank You, Jesus. Amen."

Romans 10:9 If you declare with your mouth, "Jesus is Lord," and believe in your heart that God raised him from the dead, you will be saved.

Your next step is to let someone know what you have said and to connect into a Bible-believing church. I would welcome any concerns or questions from you. Please get in touch with me at www.meredithswift.org or email me at meredith@meredithswift.org.

DEDICATION

First and foremost, I dedicate this book to my Lord Jesus and my Heavenly Father. The transforming love and freedom that I have found since I accepted the gift of salvation is so pure and precious. My life has been changed in ways that are written about in this book but also in ways I cannot even begin to describe. I give all the praise and glory for these words to my Creator.

I dedicate this book also to my wonderful family and friends. I am truly blessed to have all of these precious people in my life.

I dedicate and give thanks to my fantastic launch team and to Pardon and Elenah Kangara and the team at Palace of Writers for all their help in getting this book published.

And last, but not least, I dedicate this book to you, dear reader. I hope and pray that you have been blessed, encouraged and inspired by my story.

REFERENCES AND RESOURCES

"The Critical Journey – Stages in the Life of Faith" by Janet O. Hagberg and Robert A. Guelich, 2nd Edition, Sheffield Publishing Company, Salem Wisconsin (1995).

"Keys to Healing", by John Mellor, Tyndale House Publishers Inc., Wheaton, Illinois (1996).

"The Case for Christ – A Journalist's Personal Investigation of the Evidence for Jesus," by Lee Strobel, Zondervan (1998).

New Spirit-Filled Life Bible, New King James Version, Thomas Nelson Inc. (2002).

"Dealing with Python: Spirit of Constriction": Strategies for the Threshold #1 by Anne Hamilton, Armour Books, Corinda, Queensland, Australia (2017).

ABOUT THE AUTHOR

As you know by now, Jesus is the Lord of my life. As part of my walk with Him, I have been blessed to meet many wonderful brothers and sisters in Christ, both in Australia and around the world.

I am an introverted extrovert—I love my alone time but also my time around people. My favourite pastimes are reading, writing, cooking, gardening, listening to music and walking. I also enjoy spending time with friends and family.

Home is Townsville in sunny Far North Queensland, Australia, where I live with my younger daughter and assorted pets. My older daughter lives close by in her own home, supported 24/7 by a team of wonderful Lifestyle Assistants.

"From New Age to New Creation – Set Free" is my second book.

My first book is a devotional journey of encouragement – *"Hearing His Voice: Meeting Jesus in the Garden of Promise"*. This book was awarded the Gold Medal in the Christian Devotion/Study section of the Readers Favourite International Book Reviews and Award Contest for 2018.

You can read my blog and visit my website at: www.meredithswift.org

If you enjoyed this book and would like to leave an honest review, this would be very much appreciated. Reviews help writers get their books noticed. It doesn't have to be long—one or two sentences is perfectly okay.

God's richest blessings to you!

www.ingramcontent.com/pod-product-compliance
Lightning Source LLC
Chambersburg PA
CBHW072055290426
44110CB00014B/1694